D0439752

Statue of Liberty–Ellis Island Centennial Series

Board of Editors

Roger Daniels, Chair (University of Cincinnati)
Jay P. Dolan (University of Notre Dame)
Victor Greene (University of Wisconsin–Milwaukee)

*A list of books in the series appears
at the back of this book.*

Good-bye, Piccadilly

Good-bye, Piccadilly

BRITISH WAR BRIDES
IN AMERICA

Jenel Virden

University of Illinois Press   Urbana and Chicago

Publication of this book was supported by a grant from
the Ellis Island–Statue of Liberty Foundation.

© 1996 by the Board of Trustees of the University of Illinois
Manufactured in the United States of America
1 2 3 4 5 C P 5 4 3 2 1

This book is printed on acid-free paper.

Library of Congress Cataloging-in-Publication Data

Virden, Jenel.
    Good-bye, Piccadilly : British war brides in America / Jenel
Virden.
        p.   cm. — (Statue of Liberty–Ellis Island centennial series)
    Includes bibliographical references and index.
    ISBN 0-252-02225-4 (alk. paper). — ISBN 0-252-06528-X (pbk. :
alk. paper)
    1. World War, 1939–1945—Women—Great Britain. 2. War brides—
Great Britain—History—20th century. 3. Women immigrants—United
States—History—20th century. 4. British Americans—Cultural
assimilation. I. Title. II. Series.
D810.W7V57   1996
940.53'15042—dc20   95-4415
                                                                      CIP

To my parents,
Kenneth and Peggy Virden

Contents

Acknowledgments

This book combines archival sources with firsthand accounts and, as such, owes much to the women who agreed to be interviewed. Sybil Afdem, Eileen Cowan, Rosa Ebsary, Ivy Hammers, Mavis Olson, Joyce Osnes, June Porter, Joan Posthuma, Margaret Rippe, and Molly Tagart gave unstintingly of their time and hospitality, as did Ted Hammers and Bob Cowan, husbands of two of the women. I owe the largest debt to my mother, Peggy Virden, for starting me on the path of this research. Unfortunately, she did not live to see my conclusions in print. I like to think she would have been pleased with the final results.

I would like to acknowledge my debt to the anonymous war brides and former GIs who either filled out questionnaires or wrote to me. Some correspondents were especially helpful in supplying documents as well as encouragement. For this I thank particularly Betty Arrieta, Barbara Ashbaugh, Barbara Bauman, Veronica Fowler, June Harris, Vera Cracknell Long, Alexina Pletz, Esme Stelly, and Pamela Winfield. If I have inadvertently omitted anyone, I extend my apologies and my thanks.

Numerous professional colleagues offered support and advice that made this book a better piece of scholarship. I am indebted to Otis Pease; Philip Taylor; Susan Armitage; the anonymous readers of my manuscript; Roger Daniels, editor of the Statue of Liberty–Ellis Island Centennial Series; Richard Wentworth, director of the University of Illinois Press; and Carol Bolton Betts, an excellent copy editor. As with any research endeavor, however, I take full responsibility for any errors or inaccuracies.

I was fortunate in encountering helpful staff members at each of the archives I visited, including the National Archives in Washington, D.C.; the archives at the University of Washington in Seattle; the Public Record Office in Kew; and the Mass Observation Archives in

Sussex. The Transatlantic Brides and Parents Association membership helped me gain a clearer understanding of the war bride experience. Funding for my research came from several sources over many years, but I would like especially to thank Washington State University, the University of Washington, the Seattle branch of the English-Speaking Union, and the University of Hull.

My family and friends reside across oceans and continents, so it is impossible for me to list in the confines of this space all of the people who have contributed to my professional and personal development. To all of them, thank you; and I promise to write more letters.

1

Neglected Voices

It's a long way to Tipperary,
It's a long way to go;
It's a long way to Tipperary,
To the sweetest girl I know;
Good-bye, Piccadilly,
Farewell, Leicester Square;
It's a long, long way to Tipperary,
But my heart's right there.

British war brides are a clearly defined group within a sharply defined time. They comprised the largest single group of female immigrants to the United States in the 1940s; seventy thousand women fit this category, outnumbering war brides from all other countries. Yet, curiously, their story has been neglected by immigration research. The words "British war brides" describe women who met American GIs stationed in Great Britain in the Second World War and then married and immigrated to the United States, as well as fiancées of GIs who traveled to the States, married, and became permanent residents. Unlike the cases of other groups of immigrants, the number of British war brides in America did not increase once the war was over and GIs left Britain.

Although the women came to the United States from all parts of the British Isles, they formed an unusually homogeneous immigrant group. The majority were young (an average age of twenty-three upon arrival in the United States), had completed mandatory schooling to the age of fourteen, and came from working- or lower-middle-class families. Their gender dictated much of their experience and they emigrated alone, since they had married or were about to be married into American society. They did not settle in ethnic enclaves because they came as an act of marriage to an American citizen. Unlike some other immigrants in America, British war brides did not move into an existing immigrant population.

The immigrant experience of British war brides was unique for other reasons as well. The women were the target of some of the first special, nonrestrictive legislation in twentieth-century America. Their experience was considerably different from that of previous immigrants, for they received public welcomes and vast amounts of publicity upon their arrival in the United States. Despite all of these unparalleled features, however, British war brides also had commonalities with other immigrant groups, including a strong ethnic identity. Recent research indicates that, even though these women have lived in the United States for fifty years, the majority of them maintain a strong affiliation with Britain and have not become fully assimilated.

Part of the problem in discourse on assimilation is the lack of consensus among scholars concerning the definition of terms. Research conducted in numerous fields such as history, sociology, and anthropology, while adding to the rich data on the immigrant experience, has also made agreement on ideas about immigrants more difficult. In the present study the idea of assimilation is divided into two separate stages: cultural assimilation, or outward signs of how the immigrant adapts to the dominant culture within America; and conceptual assimilation, or the immigrants' views of their own ethnicity. Processes such as assimilation have numerous sequences that add to the problem of classification. For instance, the initial stage of immigration may produce a period of extreme difficulty even while the immigrant adapts to everyday circumstances. The story of British war brides' immigration and their residence in the United States for the last fifty years documents the complex nature of the assimilation process. It also demonstrates the persistence of ethnicity and cultural identity in immigrant groups long resident in America.

The total number of all war brides in World War II was approximately 115,000.[1] By U.S. government standards, this figure includes all people—women, men, and children—who entered the United States under the provisions of both the War Brides Act of 1945 and the Alien Fiancees and Fiances Act of 1946. However, the precise number of true war brides is difficult to determine, in part because of the variety of methods of transportation and the diverse categories of entry into the United States. The example of British war brides illustrates the complexity of determining accurate statistics. The number of war brides reported in official United States Army documents does not include those women who managed to obtain commercial passage, circumventing the army transportation process (see chapter 4). The status of fiancées in official records is also uncertain. Did they all come to the United States under the provisions of the

Fiancees Act, or did some of them arrive before June 1946 as "visitors"? An additional complication is that many of the earliest estimates of the number of British war brides did not set apart children, so overall numbers reflect women *and* children rather than solely British war brides.

Agencies involved in the transportation network had difficulty agreeing on the numbers at the time. In July 1945, American Red Cross representatives met with members of the "State, War, and Navy Departments, [and] Bureau of Immigration and Naturalization . . . [and] figures were presented by War and Navy which did not agree with State Department figures."[2] While the American Red Cross estimated the number of British war brides at between 40,000 and 60,000, its officials also admitted "it has been established that none of these agencies has definite figures, that no records are maintained here, and that the presumption is that even the theatre commanders do not have any definite information as to the number of War Brides."[3] In a 1989 survey of British war brides, 17 percent listed the location of their weddings as cities in the United States.[4] This percentage of fiancées, if projectable to the larger figure for war brides, would suggest that the official calculations of British war bride numbers were incorrect.

When the war bride transportation system got underway, far fewer war brides entered the army network than agencies had projected. Determining the exact number of British war brides of World War II who immigrated to the United States is difficult. Documents referring to "war brides" very quickly changed reference to "dependents," to acknowledge the large number of children accompanying their mothers to the United States. The army transportation records show 35,189 dependent *adults* shipped from the United Kingdom base from 8 May 1945 to 30 June 1946, along with 13,073 children. United States immigration figures indicate 34,944 British women arrived in the United States from 30 June 1946 to the end of 1950 under the War Brides Act. These two sources suggest the total British war bride immigrant population was 70,133.[5] It is possible that these two sources overlap for the period of June 1946, which would lower the overall numbers. However, it is also possible that these figures do not include fiancées, women traveling by other means, and/or women arriving in the United States outside the War Brides or Fiancees Acts. Approximately 25 percent of the war brides in the 1989 survey did not take free government transportation. Clearly, any statistics on the total number of British war brides can only be estimates; however, 70,000 seems a reasonable conclusion given available sources.

The number of British war brides is only a small part of the story, however. The phenomenon of these war brides also involves two distinct elements of immigration: the female immigrant experience and emigration from Great Britain. This study of British war brides of World War II provides insight into both of these subjects. Scholarship about British war brides is missing from the historical record of immigration, although some books do exist that chronicle the war bride experience. The majority of accounts take the form of "memoirs," written by women who were war brides themselves.[6] These books usually consist of the authors' own stories, as well as the experiences other British war brides communicated to the authors through questionnaires and interviews. While personal accounts make a valuable contribution to the history of British war brides, they do not place the experiences of the British female immigrant of the 1940s within a larger historical framework.

The first context in which to view war brides is that of British immigration to the United States. Over five million people from the United Kingdom immigrated to the United States throughout American history, the third largest group behind immigrants from Germany and Italy.[7] In addition, the British were least affected by restrictions that the American government imposed on European immigration to the United States beginning in the 1920s. Twentieth-century British immigration to the United States fluctuated with minor increases right after World War II and in the 1960s, two eras associated with economic hardships in Britain and economic boom in the United States. After the Second World War, the United States offered the attraction of a stable economy and lower unemployment. Although the United States was attractive economically, it was not the primary destination of post–World War II British emigrants. The majority chose to migrate to areas within the British Commonwealth, where they could have a better chance at success without relinquishing cultural affiliation with Britain. Canada and Australia were the first and second choices of British emigrants, while the United States took third place. From 1945 to 1955 over 80 percent of British emigration went to areas of the British Commonwealth.[8]

The common language and heritage of the United States and Great Britain have meant that British immigrants in America have received relatively little scholarly attention. This is due in part to a belief that immigration and assimilation were relatively easy for people of British birth, who spoke English and came from an industrial environment. Thomas Archdeacon notes that "the British and the Scandinavians are barely discernible in American ethnic history because neither posed a serious economic, religious, political, or cultural problem."[9] The overwhelming focus on the similarities between the United States and Great Britain has led to "an underestimation of [the British people's] special characteristics and of their role in the immigration story."[10] When discussing British immigration throughout the history of the United States, it is important to note that most Britons were fleeing not social or political problems but economic ones. In this sense, like many other immigrants, they were not trying to flee from being British but rather from their standard of living. This desire to find opportunity without sacrificing cultural identity was a trait common to many immigrants. Part of the attraction of the United States for the British had to do with certain similarities in culture and society. This is clearly the case by the 1940s when, as Allan Nevins suggested, the United States and Great Britain had much in common, including various problems and gains associated with advanced industrialization and the development of welfare legislation.[11]

This commonality does not diminish the need to examine the question of British assimilation into American society, however. British immigrants, like others, experienced a sense of alienation and loneliness associated with the decision to emigrate. Charlotte Erickson notes that historians should not make the mistake of believing the transition was smooth for British immigrants. She realizes that assimilation problems could be "masked by language similarities" and that the British subject was "more exposed because his difficulties were not so apparent."[12] Certainly the coping mechanisms associated with foreign immigration were manifest by the British in the United States. For instance, British immigrants founded social and cultural clubs and organizations throughout America as a way of easing adjustment to a new society. The Episcopal church also played a role in helping British immigrants adapt to American life. Overall, however, the distinctive British culture blended well in America. It was easy enough for these two identities to mesh when the British rarely settled into separate geographic areas and American and British history and culture had so many similarities. The British also intermarried with the American population more than other immigrant groups, which meant that second-generation British-Americans quickly assimilated into American society.

Nevertheless, the researcher studying British immigration to the United States does not want to overstate the case concerning ease of assimilation. Scholars may not have focused on British ethnicity or cultural identity, but this does not mean that it was not there. The issue of immigration is complex. Though the British were the most readily accepted ethnic group to land in America, and their arrival did not generate any anti-British nativist movements, the act of immigration itself must be considered in discussions of adjustment and assimilation. Feelings of isolation and displacement can occur regardless of one's national origin. For the study of British war brides the question becomes, How did their ethnic identity affect their assimilation into American society and what, if any, problems did they encounter in the transition to their new lives in America? Careful analysis of war brides' experiences and their struggle with assimilation shows that British immigrants faced many of the same problems as other immigrant groups. They did not simply trade a midland village for a midwestern town.

The second context for the study of British war brides pertains to the female immigration experience. Early histories of immigration did not address gender in the analysis of adjustment and assimilation, but recent scholarship has begun to focus on this issue. Although it *is* possible to discuss immigration without reference to gender, any definitive statements on migration motivations, immigration experiences, and assimilation must take into account some recognition of distinct gender differences. Women, by virtue of their relationships as wives, mothers, daughters, and sisters, had wholly different immigrant experiences from men. This is true particularly of women who immigrated in the years before the appearance of feminism, when American society defined women's lives by their relationship to the domestic arena, and it is true also of women who have immigrated to the United States in recent years from more traditional cultures.

Few could argue convincingly that the immigrant experience of women was any less alienating or lonely than male immigration as Oscar Handlin discussed it in his classic work on the "uprooted." Recent discourses on female immigration have focused on specific groups in the nineteenth century, recent female migration, and general accounts of the female immigrant experience. Throughout most of the last century, when the United States maintained an open-door policy toward European immigration, female immigration often was limited by societal and cultural factors. If the whole family could not go in search of a better way of life, usually the husband, son, father, or brother would leave first and then send for the rest of the family later. In addition, temporary immigrants in search of work—known as "birds of passage"—were predominantly male. Both of these phenomena help explain two interrelated aspects of American immigration before 1920: male immigrants outnumbered females and, although whole families did migrate, women and children often traveled alone to be reunited with the family in America.

The introduction of restrictive immigration legislation in the 1920s both hurt and helped female immigrants. Certain pieces of restrictive legislation hit women harder than men. For instance, immigration inspectors could deny admission to unwed mothers or pregnant single women. If authorities denied entry to an ill child, the mother faced the prospect of remaining in America without the child or returning to her homeland. Sometimes inspectors felt compelled to ensure that women (especially single women) had appropriate housing, invoking the morality clause to keep out women of dubious moral character. With the passage of the Literacy Act in 1917, peasants and working-class people, both male and female, faced a new hurdle to immigration. Although both sexes were the target of this restrictive legislation, more often it was the woman who had the lower level of education.[13]

On the other hand, certain aspects of the restrictive immigration policies of the United States government clearly favored women. For example, the quota laws begun in 1921 cut back on overall immigration figures but gave priority to reuniting families, so wives and children of earlier male immigrants had an advantage. The 1924 Quota Law established a preference system that worked to rank quota and nonquota immigrants. Nonquota immigrants included migrants from the Western Hemisphere, wives and children of American citizens, students, and American women who had lost citizenship by marriage to an alien. Fifty percent of the quota went to parents of American citizens and to skilled agricultural workers and their families while the next preferred group included wives and unmarried children of aliens living in the United States. The rest of the quota went to smaller groups, such as families of noncitizen members of the United States armed services.[14] The legislative changes in the 1920s partly explain the shift in male-to-female immigration ratios since the 1930s. Uniquely, World War II war brides prompted legislation that eliminated restrictions on immigration of a large category of women. British war brides, and some foreign-born husbands, entered the United States as nonquota immigrants under provision of the 1945 War Brides Act. The Alien Fiancees and Fiances Act of 1946 allowed foreign women to enter the United States as nonimmigrants.

The immigration of married women raises several interrelated issues. As in earlier immigration, married women who migrated usually followed immigrant husbands who had already crossed the Atlantic to the United States. If the separation had been especially lengthy, strains on the marriage itself may have developed. The letters of female immigrants often reflected a concern, even clear desperation, over abandonment.[15] Women remembered this separation as a time of great concern over the welfare of their husbands as well as one of questions about the faithfulness of their spouses. If communication was slow, women went for long periods of time without hearing from husbands who were "worlds" away. Other problems, such as bigamy, also arose. Doris Weatherford reported that some male immigrants conveniently forgot marriages in their homelands as they contracted new marriages in America. The problem prompted one sociologist to recommend that the United States government establish a formal, comprehensive immigration policy related to abandonment, bigamy, and divorce.[16] Some British war brides of World War II confronted the same problems.

Separation also meant that partners no longer shared experiences. Hence, when they reunited, both had been changed by outside events. For most immigrants the process of conforming to a new culture begins immediately upon arrival. In the case of married couples where the husband had immigrated first, this process had already begun for him while his wife was in the "old" country. A wife arriving in the United States might discover that her husband no longer resembled the man she had wed. His cultural assimilation could be manifest in anything from the adoption of American-style dress to a disregard for traditional values of the "old world." The married female immigrant might find that her mate personified the enormity of the move she had made from one culture to the next, from one world to another.[17] The cultural distance between husband and wife was magnified for war brides. Unlike other female immigrants, British war brides had married into American society. Therefore, their husbands were at home in their environment while the women faced the transition to a new culture.

Once in the United States, the married female immigrant's life often revolved around her domestic role of wife and mother. Since migration usually shifted the family context from an extended family network in the homeland to a nuclear family in America, the female immigrant faced questions involving the family without the aid of a support network. Hence, a married woman immigrating to the United States might face a sense of loss of control in her relationships to her husband, her children, and her extended family.[18] While some war brides' families joined them in the United States later, the majority of the women confronted adjustments to marriage, childbirth, and child care without recourse to a female family network.

There are two opposing views on the question of assimilation and the female immigrant. One group of researchers suggests that women adjusted better than men to the new culture, pointing to the lower return rates for female immigrants. However, men migrated primarily for work opportunities while women were more likely to immigrate as a part of family reunification. Female immigration, therefore, would more often be a permanent decision associated with the relocation of "home" rather than a temporary move for economic gain, perhaps making adjustment easier.[19] The other side argues that female immigrants had a harder time assimilating than men; they faced isolation because their ties to the home generated less contact with the new culture.[20] This argument would suggest that female immigrants stayed home. However, recent research on contemporary female immigration indicates that more immigrant women worked outside the home than previously supposed. In some cases foreign women interacted in the new culture more than their male partners due to the nature of the paid work they performed, especially in the lower-paid service industries. Obviously, numerous factors influence the process of assimilation. What is certain is that the female immigrant experience differs from the male experience due in large part to women's and men's differing gender roles.

A related factor in immigrant adjustment is the availability or proximity of people functioning under the same circumstances or pressures. Most immigrants, male or female, sought out fellow immigrants in one way or another. Immigrant neighborhoods played a major part in easing feelings of alienation and loneliness. For some female immigrants, coping with changes associated with migration led to the creation of women's clubs. Maxine Schwartz Seller, in her book *Immigrant Women*, suggests that female immigrants did not have extended family networks to help them with problems traditionally associated with the female sphere, such as childbirth and child care. Hence, many female immigrants formed clubs that brought women of similar cultures together for companionship and support on both the local and national levels. These women joined forces for a variety of reasons, including the need to discuss topics such as education, language difficulties, or employment.[21] For British war brides the lack of family support networks or distinct ethnic communities had an impact on their adjustment to life in the United States. As female immigrants marrying into American society, they also confronted problems linked to their gender. British war brides formed and joined clubs based on their circumstances as immigrants. Membership in these clubs brought them together with women in similar situations.

Immigration research also looks at the "pull factors" that attract immigrants to the United States. What could cause a person to decide that leaving home was preferable to staying? Seller suggests that "the societies from which . . . immigrant women came had one thing in common. All were experiencing far-reaching economic and social changes, changes that set large numbers of people in motion."[22] This is true for most of nineteenth-century European immigration related to the industrial revolution and overpopulation and for the early twentieth-century migrations associated with economic depression and war. The question of immigration motivation for war brides encompasses both marriage relationships and the framework of a society in flux due to the economic and social upheavals of war. A peripheral issue, then, is the question of the impact of war on society. Many historians have examined British society during the Second World War and the resultant changes in sexual behavior. Admittedly, the constant threat of death played a role in the development of relationships. However, the study of a select group of participants in the war, namely British war brides and American GIs, reveals that these couples came together and married despite the war, not because of it.

Finally, for some immigrants, the image of the United States played a major part in their decision to come to America. The United States had an expanding economy throughout most of the nineteenth and twentieth centuries, and immigrants' letters from the United States often reflected a faith in the potential for economic improvement in America compared with economic hardships in the homeland. In addition, the ideal of America as a land of possibilities fired the imagination of some immigrants. What prompted the British war bride to emigrate? Was it only a choice of the heart or was there an economic motivation behind the war bride phenomenon? While the image of America held by most British war brides proved inaccurate, research indicates that the immigration motivation for the majority of British war brides was personal, not economic.

The war bride story encompasses many of the complex issues surrounding immigration and assimilation processes. The tale of these women is a part of both immigration and social history. It fills in many gaps in information on British immigration, war as a factor in migration, and the problems and strains of the immigrant experience. Despite the large number of British war brides and the myriad issues their immigration touches upon, their story has been neglected. Until now the voices of these immigrants, as Britons and as women, have gone unheard.

2

The Second World War in Britain

I always used to say that if there was another war, people here would never understand it. . . . I think that was a great disillusionment for a lot of young people. I mean there was so much unfaithfulness. It wasn't Americans only, it was British. I came to the conclusion that there was no such thing as a faithful husband given the time and opportunity, or vice versa.

—Rosa Ebsary

British war brides as a group led unusual lives. They were, on average, just sixteen years old when war erupted in Europe in 1939, but most had been out of school for two years. The confluence of events in Britain in the 1940s provided a unique experience for these women. Throughout the 1930s, British society had contended with the economic problems of the depression, and it was further disrupted by the outbreak of war. British war brides were becoming young adults at an uncertain time. Yet old values persisted, and most British women anticipated that, despite fluctuating circumstances, they would eventually marry and raise families. The only alteration the war brought to this expected scenario of women's domestic role was the nationality of the men they married.

THE WOMEN

An examination of British women's lives in the 1930s and 1940s underlies any understanding of war bride immigration to the United States. We must ask how World War II affected the women and their expectations. Most of the historical research about the impact of the war on British women centers on the question of whether the war itself acted as a mechanism of permanent change. Some historians suggest that the war hastened the move toward a more democratic society in both Britain and the United States. They contend that the overall impact of the war was to change women's lives permanently by bringing more women into the work force and breaking down barriers that women had been unable to breach before the war. The other side argues that World War II really had little effect on women's lives. Partisans of this view suggest that, although the war initiated marked transformation in women's work and society's rigid gender spheres, any shift was only temporary, or "for the duration." This line of reasoning maintains that the postwar world looked much the same for women as had the prewar world and that it was not until the 1960s and the feminist movement that women experienced any real transformation.[1] Both sides do agree, however, that from 1939 to 1945 women's lives were distinctly different from their lives before or after the war.

In Britain in the 1930s a person's class and gender influenced his or her experiences. Both factors affected schooling, employment, and expectations. Expectations of a woman's role in society in prewar Britain, however, were remarkably classless. A middle- or working-class woman might work for a while before marriage but her future remained tied to marriage and the household. The earliest point when students could discontinue their education was at fourteen, otherwise known as the "school-leaving age." In the 1930s only 15 percent of British girls continued their education beyond that.[2] The immediate post-school years entailed paid work for the majority of single, young women. Many employment opportunities for women depended on class status and geographic location. Large cities were witnessing an increased demand for female workers to fill clerical and sales positions. There was also a heightened demand for female labor in light manufacturing, while the textile industry dominated female employment in the northern part of England. Domestic work opportunities were on the rise throughout Britain in the 1930s, although a shift was occurring away from private households and toward businesses.

While the depression years witnessed an increase in the number of working women as more women sought ways to supplement household incomes, the majority of married women in Britain did not work outside the home before the Second World War. Fully 90 percent of married women were not in paid, full-time work in 1931.[3] Wages for women workers in prewar Britain were lower overall than for men, in part due to the nature of female work (skilled versus unskilled labor) and in part due to society's view that female labor was a temporary, and therefore less important, presence in the marketplace.

While British society in the 1930s might have included a number of women working outside the home, the expectations of most women revolved around marriage and motherhood.

By 1938 the British government had to confront the issue of female employment as part of its mobilization for total war. The government formed several female service organizations in the early war years, including the Women's Volunteer Service (WVS—Civil Defense), Women's Auxiliary Air Force (WAAF), Auxiliary Territorial Service (ATS), Women's Royal Navy Service (WRNS), and Women's Land Army (WLA). The mobilization of women for war work took a bit longer, but it occurred far more quickly than in World War I. Part of the British government's problem was an inherent dislike of calling on women. Any government actions necessitated by war had the potential to cause long-term changes in British society. A fear of drastic change could explain the British government's slow pace of female mobilization and its decision to couch female recruitment in terms that maintained gender spheres. For instance, the government stressed that the mobilization of women was for the duration only and used terms drawn from the domestic sphere to describe many of the women's jobs.[4]

Not until March 1941 did the British government require all women between nineteen and forty years of age to register their jobs with the local Employment Exchange run by the Ministry of Labour. The government extended the age limit to forty-five in 1942 and to fifty in 1943.[5] The ministry hoped to direct women into industries that were suffering from labor shortages; however, compulsory job placement occurred only if the woman was not already "employed to advantage."[6] Other government acts followed, including the National Service #2 Act, of December 1941, which called for conscription or "liability for service" of single women age twenty to thirty beginning in January 1942. The Employment of Women Order in February 1942 called for all women age twenty to thirty to seek employment only through Employment Exchanges.[7]

At first glance it appears that the government was taking steps to mobilize and organize the entire female population of Britain. However, it continued to distinguish between single and married women by allowing a number of exemptions to service that emphasized women's roles within the household. The government gave classification priority to "mobile" women who were single, twenty to twenty-one years of age, without household responsibilities, and not in school. Any woman with responsibilities, who fit within the Household R category, was exempt. This category included any woman who: was running a household with two or more residents other than herself; was running a household with herself and one other if the other person was her father, husband, or brother; was helping her mother in her household; or had young children of her own.[8] By trying to fill wartime labor needs with young, single, "mobile" women, the government regulations clearly attempted to keep out of the work force those women who were already following traditional paths.

The British government never developed fully its conscription of women into industry or the armed services and continued to maintain a myriad of exemptions directly related to gender roles. In addition, the government was reluctant to back legislation that might initiate long-lasting change such as government funded day-care. The British government did not provide day-care for working mothers, preferring to promote the idea of child "minders"; working women had to rely upon friends or relatives to look after their children.[9] Hence, women felt the double burden of work within and outside the home. With the arrival of wartime rationing, the phenomenon of enemy bombing, and the government call to female employment, women's duties took on nightmarish dimensions. The statistics compiled by Mass Observation, a social survey organization, reflected these problems associated with shopping and child care. It was reported that 62 percent of married women workers and 45 percent of single women gave excuses other than illness for absenteeism, such as responsibilities for the home, shopping, and child care. However, only 1 percent of working men gave these responses.[10]

In 1943 the Ministry of Labour finally began advocating the use of part-time female workers. Many women had complained that, as wives and mothers, they were unable to hold full-time paid jobs and maintain their households despite a publicity push to get women to contribute to the war effort. Women had been asking the government to formulate part-time employment plans for some time. When the government responded, it is unclear whether it acted out of a concern for the needs of women or, more likely, was willing to advocate part-time work only when faced with a labor shortage. Women lobbied for part-time work because they were under a great deal of pressure to help in the war effort, often in inconsistent ways. Government agencies urged women, variously and contradictorily, to evacuate their homes, stay and fight, work outside the home, keep the home fires burning, take nontraditional jobs, and maintain the sanctity of the traditional female gender sphere. Much of this inconsistent public pressure could help explain why certain women suffered a sense of frustration and uncertainty. Some historians argue that the call to work in factories afforded women unprecedented opportunity while others suggest that the government's publicity campaign reinforced women's traditional gender roles and second-rate economic status.

Rate of pay and the numbers of women engaged in outside work provide a means of analyzing the changing status of British women during World War II. One result of the mobilization of women in Britain was a shift in the gender ratio of employment. The most substantial change in female employment occurred in the number of married women working. Women's wages also rose but the ratio of female to male wage rate changed only slightly. The percentage of women in the work force rose by only 1 percent by 1951 compared to 1931 (see table 1). Clearly, the number of married women increased. However, any assessment of the apparent wartime gains for British women in employment and income must also take into account the small percentage of women who joined the trade unions (25 percent), where real labor power lay. As one author has suggested, the British women the government recruited were not harbingers of a new social order; their wartime roles turned out to be "temporary, expedient, and reversible."[11]

Other dimensions of the effect of the war on British women are harder to quantify but no less important. As seen earlier, the British government was reluctant to embrace a philosophy toward women that modified the traditional role of women as wives and mothers. Even though the government felt compelled to place women in the labor market as a solution to the shortage occasioned by the war, many people responded to this nontraditional circumstance by suggesting that women who did move into these roles were somehow suspect. One of the problems job recruiters faced, in both industry and the armed services, was the public's assumption that women who

Table 1. Female Working Population

Year	Single, Widowed, Divorced (%)	Married (%)	Percent of Work Force	Percent Wage of Males
1931	84	16	29.8	47*
1943–44	56	43	38.8	51
1951	57	43	30.8	

*From October 1938.

Source: Summerfield, *Women Workers*, Appendix B.

served in nontraditional fields were of questionable moral character. Traditionalists believed that female factory workers were lower class and of loose moral makeup; this reputation followed the military branches as well, especially the ATS. Eileen Cowan recalled this attitude as it related to her decision to join the military when she noted that "when friends knew that I was going to join the army, they said, 'Oh you shouldn't do that because the girls in the army, they're really loose girls.' I said, 'Hey, just because I'm putting on a uniform . . .' You know I was in the army for over three years and of all the girls I met none of them ever got pregnant."[12] Indeed, the ATS had a far lower pregnancy rate than the general civilian population.[13] Unfortunately, the truth did not keep amateur poets from suggesting such recruitment slogans as "Up with a lark and to bed with a WRN" for the women's navy, or "Backs to the Land" for the WLA.[14] Some objections to women in uniform revolved around concerns about women's femininity. A letter to the editor of the London *News Chronicle* in March 1940, commenting on female service personnel, suggested, "It is clear enough that far too much time and money is wasted on sheer non-essential work and military display. Too much time is wasted in attempting to dewomanise women."[15] Mass Observation conducted research into men's attitudes toward the ATS in January 1941 and this concern surfaced often. One man commented that he would not want his wife to join the armed services and noted that "the A.T.S. movement can only mean regimentation, removal of individuality and destruction of femininity."[16]

The gains of British women during World War II, in work and pay, may seem ambiguous but the war had a social and emotional impact on these individuals. The war produced a more open and less restrictive social climate. The combination of outside paid work, increased wages, and wartime changes afforded the women more independence and resources to enjoy more leisure-time activities. The move toward a less rigid social and moral order helped to free up the atmosphere in which the young women of Britain came to maturity. Sybil Afdem, who joined the army, reminisced that the war had changed her life by opening unexpected horizons. She confessed that she "was one of those real meek, mild children. I often wonder what would have become of me if the war hadn't come along and the army hadn't taken me away from home. I often wonder how I would have turned out. Probably my mother would have picked out some suitable fellow. That was the making of me really, going into the army. My mother thought it was the ruin of me."[17] Ninety-six percent of the war brides in the 1989 survey worked during the war in a wide range of jobs. This statistic reflects the British government's decision to target young, single women. They filled positions as armed services personnel (24 percent, including the WLA), secretaries, factory laborers, civil servants, shop assistants, and, less frequently, teachers and nurses. British women were ready to take advantage of the unique opportunities presented by the conduct of total war. It was this situation into which the American GIs arrived.

THE MEN

American GIs began arriving in the United Kingdom in January 1942. Approximately twenty thousand Americans were already serving in various British armed services, most notably the Eagle Squadron of the Royal Air Force. However, the major influx of Americans into the British Isles occurred after December 1941, when Pearl Harbor was attacked. The number of GIs in the United Kingdom at any one time fluctuated according to the strategic battles of the war; for instance, the number increased just before the North African invasion in November 1942 and peaked to a record 1.6 million before the Normandy invasion in June 1944. Of the 4.5 million GIs sent to Europe during the war, 3 million passed through or served in Britain.[18] Many Americans served at permanent duty stations in the United Kingdom, acting as support services for the allied forces in the European Theater of Operations (ETO) throughout the wartime period.

The average age of the men in the American army during World War II was twenty-six. The average age was lower in the other branches of the service; twenty-three years for the navy and twenty-two in the marines.[19] An American GI was likely to have completed one year of high school, a figure considerably higher than the World War I average of sixth grade. In addition, most GIs were on their first overseas trip and, as one veteran explained, the prospect was both terrifying and exhilarating:

> If you were a serviceman going overseas in World War II, you were presumed by the folks at home to be a warrior who by the very act of going had already become something of a hero. . . . To have revealed that you were actually eager and excited and a little bit frightened would have been "square" and embarrassingly improper for the kind of laconic, hard-bitten troopers you and your fellow pink-cheeked military fledglings liked to think you had become. But even though you concealed it under a pretended indifference, the excitement was there. You were at

the age of adventure, as interested in new things as a half-grown pup, probably had traveled very little before going into military service, and now you were on your way to some exotic faraway place you had never expected to see.[20]

Most Britons welcomed the GIs in 1942 as symbols of America's new involvement in the struggle against Hitler and the hope for a swifter end to the war. The GIs, however, like Benjamin Franklin's fish and visitors, were often less welcome the longer they stayed. The British public's reaction to GIs varied along lines of age and sex; the Americans usually got along well with children. Many Britons today have fond memories of being the "gum-chum" of an American.

Perhaps the best description of Americans, from the British perspective, was that they were unorthodox. American soldiers could be very generous but this generosity elicited a variety of reactions. Some Britons saw this as an endearing quality while others complained of the waste and excesses that GIs seemed to promote. One problem was that American GIs were willing to pay a high price for services, which disadvantaged the native population. The Americans usually overspent on shoe shines, haircuts, and laundry. This tendency of the Americans to "burn their money" left the average Londoner with the complaint that the providers of these services were "turning their noses at old customers to give preference to Americans."[21] One American veteran, Ted Hammers, recalling his first night out in Britain, admitted, "I had to bribe the local tailor with cigarettes even though I didn't smoke, to get him to do my uniform because we only had the uniforms we came in. The rest were in our bags and were coming on the boats and we wanted to go to this shindig that night. So I had to bribe this guy to clean my uniform and press it the best he could so I could look decent."[22]

One wartime Mass Observation correspondent noted that "public feeling regarding the Americans varies considerably. The majority feel kindly towards them, and think them a friendly and generous lot."[23] GIs could often find themselves treated to free drinks at the pub or a dinner of shared rations with a British family, and many found ways to reciprocate. American military officials suggested that GIs take food to their hosts. Joan Posthuma remembered that her future husband brought army food to help with the rationing at her home. She recalled, "When he came home sometimes he would bring a pound of butter, and I know oftentimes [the military] used to throw out the Spam. Instead of throwing it out they would leave it and then anybody who wanted it could take it. My husband often brought a great big hunk of Spam home, especially after [his friends] knew we were married. And sometimes peaches. [The GIs] were told that if they could carry it they could bring it home. We had Spam, Spam, Spam, Spam but it was a blessing."[24]

Conversely, other Britons viewed American behavior as aggressive, pushy, immoral, and scandalous. A British subject noted that "the yarn that is going about . . . to the effect that the Yanks have no use for anything they cannot drink or seduce has its roots in their behaviour. . . . In their actual intercourse they are completely without shame. I do not think anyone would be surprised to see a Yank having a girl in the middle of the street."[25] June Porter from Gloucester remembered that her parents were shocked by Americans stationed nearby. She recalled that there was an American camp "at the base of the hill where, since I was a little child, on Sundays you always went for a walk. You would go for your Sunday walk and you would see them up the hill, lying in the grass with the girls. My mother's generation thought this was awful while we were intrigued. They pitched little tents up in the corner. I didn't think *that* could be going on, but my parent's age group just thought it was awful."[26]

A *Time* magazine article in December 1943 outlined the ways in which GIs got in trouble in England. The most frequent charges brought against the GIs by the U.S. Army included: drunkenness, consorting with prostitutes, nonregulation uniform, failure to salute, unauthorized use of vehicles, no identification, no pass, ignoring the blackout, and necking in doorways. The article reported, "In recent months it has become increasingly obvious that the people of Britain are annoyed by the free-spending, free-loving, free-speaking U.S. troops. . . . Britons have now come to think of the U.S. soldier as sloppy, conceited, insensitive, undiscriminating, noisy."[27] The article, written for an American audience, went on to assure the folks back home that there was really nothing to worry about since the American GI was just acting much the same as the British Tommy in World War I in France, thereby implying that one can expect various cultural clashes during world wars with resident allies. Other publications, for GI eyes, repeated the list of offenses *Time* had outlined. *Stars and Stripes* added the warning that Americans could easily find themselves in trouble by throwing around their money and by picking fights. Not only could the GI fall victim to bad booze and potential muggers, according to the army, the American soldier could also further damage relations with the British people by his conduct. A clearly "wise practice is to steer clear of becoming involved in arguments with civilians or soldiers of other nations in public houses."[28]

The American soldier apparently needed constant reminding about how to behave, despite the distribution of *A Short Guide to Great Britain,* a military "how-to" book issued by the War and Navy Departments in mid-1942. Targeted to all American servicemen on their way to or already resident in the United Kingdom, the guide outlined exactly what they could expect to find in Great Britain and how they should behave there. The pamphlet briefly described the geography, climate, language, and currency, but this was not the focus of the United States government's message. American authorities wanted the GI to act like a guest in a war-torn country, remembering that Britain had been suffering through total war for several years. While the guide insisted that American and British people were alike, it warned the GIs about bragging and showing off, which would readily set them apart from their comparatively reserved and understated hosts. The publication advised GIs to remember that "the English language didn't spread across the oceans and over the mountains and jungles and swamps of the world because these people were panty-waists." To "get along," the army suggested that Americans should accept differences, rather than criticize, especially the differences that seemed hardest to understand by American standards. These differences included such phenomena as driving on the "wrong" side of the road, the "impossible" monetary system, and the ubiquitous "warm beer."[29] The guide even included a section on British women in uniform that admonished the American servicemen to respect the uniform and the rank regardless of gender. The GIs needed reminding that "when you see a girl in khaki or air-force blue with a bit of ribbon on her tunic—remember she didn't get it for knitting more socks than anyone else in Ipswich." In addition, the army suggested that the average British subject had seen more action so far in the war than most American soldiers, so GIs should treat the citizens with respect and not act like war heroes.

The British government also attempted to ward off trouble between the British and the Americans by issuing its own pamphlet, *Meet the Americans.* It reiterated much of the same information as the GI guide, only from the British perspective. The British publication emphasized the importance of "getting along" with one's allies to win the war. Be patient and respectful, it advised, and get to know the Americans. Mass Observation conducted several inquiries into attitudes toward the Americans throughout the war years. Only 27 percent of the British public expressed favorable remarks in 1940 when Britain was facing Hitler alone. Interestingly, the overall favorable rating of GIs rose when American initiated Lend Lease and again when Japan bombed Pearl Harbor. However, the approval ratings dropped to 34 percent in 1943, after the GIs had resided in Britain for a year. The American traits the British liked least were boastfulness and materialism. What the British liked most were American generosity and frankness.[30]

The American GIs had their own opinions of the British. The GIs generally liked the British people and the pubs. While the British might comment on GI morality, the servicemen had their own opinions on that topic as well. Mass Observation conducted an indirect poll of Americans in London in March 1943 to find out what the GIs thought about their host country. While two soldiers commented that what they liked best were the London prostitutes known as "Piccadilly Commandos," the majority of men had a more unfavorable attitude toward the moral climate. One GI noted that he did not "think too much of the morals of Englishwomen, and the married ones are the worst"; another said that "the sex morals in this country are very low. Our boys take advantage of it, I know, but they don't respect the women of Britain any the more for it."[31]

Clearly, the two cultures occasionally clashed despite the British and American governments' attempts to foster understanding. Two British groups who most disliked the American GIs were the British Tommies and, to a lesser extent, young male British civilians. The GI guide had warned Americans that in their relations with British troops, "two actions on your part will show up the friendship—swiping his girl, and not appreciating what his army has been up against. Yes, and rubbing it in that you are better paid than he is." The United States authorities were right when they warned of these potential areas of conflict. The American GI made approximately five times the amount of the British soldier and had all of his necessities paid for. American soldiers could afford to buy more than their allied counterparts. In 1940 United States dollars, an average GI received sixty dollars per month; a Canadian soldier, forty-five dollars; an Australian, thirty-four dollars; and a British Tommy, just twelve dollars.[32]

While higher pay was a factor in some British women's initial attraction to GIs, the character of the Americans also played a role in the development of relationships. If GIs were "overpaid, oversexed, and overfed," this was only part of the story. The American male was far more assertive in his relationships with women than was the average British man. Some British women who dated Americans described them as bold, exciting, cheeky, and gallant. June Porter remembered British men she dated as being "very polite and nice and they didn't have the money that the Yank had and they did not like the Yank for that reason . . . but the English boys didn't have that suave. It wasn't so much the money because that really wasn't what it was all about. There was something fascinating about the Americans. . . . They treated you differently. Of course there were the braggarts and what not, but the majority that I knew, they treated you very differently. You were important."[33]

The anthropologist Margaret Mead attempted to explain the attraction British women felt for Americans. She suggested that American men planning to spend a pleasant evening out would include women, whereas British men were more likely to prefer the company of other men in all matters other than sex. Mead believed that the difference between the British and American servicemen's treatment of women grew out of differences between the British public-school ideal and the American coed high school.[34] Margaret Wharton reinforced this conclusion in her book on her Wiltshire childhood when she noted that in her school "it seemed the aim and object of the authorities to keep boys and girls as completely separated as possible. We entered school through separate doors and were segregated in the classrooms. . . . Socializing, even to the extent of walking to school together, was frowned upon and the only purely social contact we had with the opposite sex was at the annual social."[35]

Whatever its origin, this cultural difference was the reason most women cited to explain the attraction of the GIs. The Americans would approach women on the streets or in stores, and would even whistle and shout out greetings from passing trucks. British women who went out with GIs often remarked on being overwhelmed by attention, such as the servicemen's holding doors and chairs for them or giving them flowers and gifts. The Americans seemed to epitomize a Hollywood image, with their cocky attitudes, their passion for dances like the jitterbug, and their paychecks. They had style. Sybil Afdem remembered dating an Englishman after having dated Americans and recalled that "he would come and get me and take me out and he was very, very proper and I didn't really care for him. He was very, very nice, very English, dull, very boring, and my mother thought he was great."[36] One GI, reporting on life in the United Kingdom for *Yank* magazine, summed up attitudes toward the GI when he noted that "the effect of Yank troops on the Irish citizenry varies considerably with the citizen's age and sex. The children are nuts about us, to slip into the vernacular. We get along very well with the girls, a fact which isn't calculated to endear us to the boys, and the older people take us pretty much as we come."[37]

Not all British women, however, were taken with the American soldiers. Rosa Ebsary was unimpressed and remembered "they all had rimless glasses and were overweight and wore white socks. They used to roll up their pants and you could see their bare legs. Of course, we thought those olive jackets and pink pants were just hilarious."[38] Some women found American manners disturbing, as suggested by the story June Porter tells of going to a restaurant in London where her GI date "ordered chicken and started picking it up with his fingers. I excused myself to go to the ladies room and I never went back."[39]

While the GIs in Britain during the war elicited a wide range of responses from Britons, American servicemen who married British women had some similarities. The majority of GI husbands in the 1989 study were members of the United States Army (92 percent), with 17 percent in the Army Air Force; only 3 percent were officers and only 5 percent were career men. Their average age, upon arrival in Great Britain, was twenty-three years, and the majority came from working- and middle-class backgrounds. These men did not expect to return to the United States with wives at war's end.

THE WAR

The question of the impact of the war on the domestic front has generated debate among historians. Some argue that the uncertainties of wartime precipitated a dramatic shift in moral behavior. Another view is held by scholars such as David Reynolds, who, in his comprehensive study of the GIs in Britain, writes that "wartime male-female relationships may not have been as exceptional as moralists believed."[40] As historians analyze the impact of World War II on society, and specifically on moral norms, they must consider how people were affected by increased mobility and by feelings of anonymity, uncertainty, and immediacy—living for the moment—in wartime. For example, in September 1939 one-third of all Britons (approximately sixteen million people) changed addresses, and over sixty million changes of address occurred in a population of thirty-five million during the war years.[41] The combination of evacuation, mobilization, and destruction of housing meant that more people were on the move within British society than ever before. This mobility brought into proximity groups and individuals who might never have had contact otherwise. This also meant that some people experienced a degree of anonymity, which could have numerous consequences. For instance, a woman in the ATS remembered that when she moved away from home, where no one knew her, she had much more freedom to act. It was easier for young women to go into a pub for a pint without fear of local gossip.[42]

During World War II, the civilian population lived with a degree of uncertainty about survival that only soldiers had known before. Traditional battle lines had effectively been eradicated by bomber aircraft. Approximately sixty thousand British civilians died from enemy action during the war years. The figure increases to eighty-two thousand if Allied personnel killed in Britain are added to the equation.[43] In the early 1940s both the civilian and military populations experienced a heightened sense of insecurity—no place was safe and no future guaranteed. There were many consequences associated with this circumstance. The phenomenon of the twenty-four-hour pass and the rush to enjoy oneself in a short time had repercussions in relationships. This sense of urgency helped to eliminate the pre-war customs of proper introductions, lengthy courtship, and waiting for marriage.

Several factors affected the development of male-female relationships during the Second World War. Most important, the young GIs and British women were at the age of developing sexual awareness. In addition, the surrounding culture and the war itself fostered a preoccupation with sex. Sexual innuendo was often the basis of the entertainment put on for the soldiers by both the United Service Organization (USO) and the Entertainments National Services Association (ENSA). Pinups and sexy comic strips were the "art" of the war; GI magazines such as *Yank* and *Stars and Stripes* popularized sexuality while aircraft and barracks boasted displays of the female body. Sexual tones came to the fore in everything from music to movies.[44]

Debate has ensued about whether there was a need to sexualize the war and reinforce gender spheres by viewing women as objects that "ratified men as male," or whether the violence and fear associated with waging war produced a need to relieve these emotions sexually.[45] Another explanation might hold that in Britain during World War II, large numbers of young men and women could meet and date without familial supervision at a time when society had more important concerns. These young people were at a stage in their lives when they were discovering their sexuality. While sex was not invented in World War II, some historians have suggested that sexual contact increased. They use the increased rates of marriage, divorce, venereal disease, and illegitimate births to illustrate their point.

From the beginning of the draft in 1940, the United States Army identified the active sex lives of its soldiers as a rapidly growing concern. Although the army had long recognized sexual activity as a potential problem, the influx of large numbers of men into the ranks during the war years increased the military's concern. The higher percentage of married GIs in the wartime army did not stop promiscuity. Military research in 1942 concerning rates of venereal disease among soldiers revealed that 75 percent of the men were having sex. Interestingly, 60 percent of women service personnel were sexually active.[46] An armed services survey in 1945 noted that the rate of sexual contact increased as time in service rose. This survey concluded that the majority of GIs who had been in the army for two or more years had "regular" sexual relations with foreign women. On average, 75 percent of all GIs engaged in sex while overseas.[47] The major concern of both the army and civilian authorities was that only 50 percent of the sexually active GIs overseas were using prophylactics. The distribution of condoms suggests that the army's attitude toward the sexual conduct of American soldiers was overshadowed by the larger concern about the rising infection rate of sexually transmitted diseases among servicemen.

Similar statistics exist for the civilian populations. The venereal disease rate in Britain began to rise at the outbreak of war in 1939 and continued through 1942 when the Yanks arrived. In the early years of the war the rate of infection for syphilis had risen in Britain for both men and women.[48] The rate of infection for British men remaining in Britain leveled off after peaking in 1942, but the rate of infection for British women continued to rise. This was due, in part, to the arrival of the American troops. The number of venereal disease cases in United States Army personnel stationed in Britain tripled by early 1943 and was three times the rate among United States troops stationed at home.[49] Stories about venereal disease in Britain and the rest of the European Theater of Operations appeared throughout the pages of the GI newspapers and magazines, especially in 1943, when the American troops were massing in Britain for the assault on the continent, and in the second half of 1945, after the war in Europe was over.

The average infected British woman was nineteen to twenty-three years old and had become infected through a single act of exposure, not because she was working as a prostitute. This combination of a major increase in the venereal disease rate and the spread of the disease to the otherwise untouched civilian population moved the British government in early 1943 to launch a massive educational campaign that brought the topic of sex and sexually transmitted diseases into the open. (See figure 1.) The result was a dramatic drop in the infection rate by spring 1944.[50] Venereal disease continued to

Figure 1. Venereal disease campaign (*Stars and Stripes,* 15 May 1943, 2). The British government's campaign against venereal disease intensified at the same time that this image appeared in the GI newspaper.

be a problem for the United States Army as American troops entered each new foreign country; a rise in the rate of infection followed allied victories.

Another indicator historians use to prove an increase in sexual contact in Britain during the war is the rate of illegitimate births. The overall wartime birth rate in Britain fell from 1939 to 1941, then began to rise, and peaked in 1944. A more interesting statistic indicates that the percentage of illegitimate conceptions legitimized by marriage declined and the number of pregnancies of married women by men other than their husbands rose during the war years. The decline in the legitimization of pregnancy may have been due to mobility caused by the war and the difficulty in arranging weddings. The transient nature of wartime relationships could also explain the decline. The number of adoptions rose, to some extent in response to conceptions between married women and men other than their husbands. The largest rise in illegitimate births occurred among women between twenty and thirty years of age.[51] The increase in overall numbers of illegitimate births, the drop in the number of illegitimate conceptions ending in marriage, the increased number of illegitimate conceptions by married women, and the shift of illegitimate births toward women twenty to thirty years old all indicate a definite change in sexual contacts. However, the overall number of births did not increase dramatically. What did change was the percentage of illegimate births, from 5.5 percent during 1934–39 to 10.4 percent during 1940–45. Hence, one could argue that sexual contact did not increase greatly but that failure to legitimize pregnancy did.[52] The rise in illegitimate births after 1942 suggests much about the relations between American GIs and British women since this rise coincided with the departure of British men to other theaters of the war and the arrival of the United States troops.

Divorce and marriage statistics offer another indication of wartime relations. Divorce had been on the increase in Britain throughout the 1930s in large part due to the relaxing of divorce law. One could expect that the war would heighten this trend, but the overall rise in gross numbers between 1939 and 1945 is extraordinary (see table 2). However, part of the increase was a backlash from the hasty marriages contracted at the start of the war by couples feeling the pressure of imminent separation while another segment of the divorce statistics reflects a backlog in the court system since the time of new legislation easing divorce restrictions. An interesting aspect of increased divorce rate statistics emerges when one examines who was filing for divorce and why. Women petitioned the courts in over 50 percent of the divorces in Britain before the war, but by 1945 husbands filed 58 percent of the divorce petitions; 75 percent of these latter cases were for adultery.[53] The divorce statistics are compelling when compared to data concerning marriages in Britain during the war. The number of marriages rose at the beginning of the war, with the peak in 1939–40. After this, the number of marriages declined to a low in 1943, then rose again by 1945.[54] The return of British troops at war's end explains part of the rise in marriage rates in 1945; the rest of the increase was due to the marriage of British women to allied servicemen after VE-Day.

Table 2. Illegitimacy, Marriage, and Divorce, 1939–45

Year	Illegitimate Births	Marriages	Divorces
1939	25,570	440,000	8,770
1940	25,633	471,000	7,139
1941	31,058	389,000	8,357
1942	36,467	370,000	12,082
1943	43,709	296,000	15,470
1944	55,173	303,000	19,035
1945	63,420	398,000	27,789
Total	281,030	2,667,000	98,642

Source: *The Registrar General's Statistical Review of England and Wales for the Six Years 1940–1945*, text, vol. 2—Civil (London: His Majesty's Stationery Office, 1951).

The war's impact, then, was manifold. What can clearly be seen is that, for the GIs and British women, World War II was an unprecedented event with particular ramifications. The average war bride was eighteen years old when the GIs arrived, which suggests much in the way of sexual awareness as well as rebelliousness and the search for independence. Joyce Osnes was an eighteen-year-old nurse-in-training in Liverpool during the war and suggested that she "loved" the nightly bombings because the hospital matrons waived the 10:00 P.M. curfew during air raids. The hospital authorities expected the trainees to seek shelter immediately rather than attempt to return to the hospital. For this young woman that meant "we could stay out until one, two, three o'clock in the morning!"[55] The war shaped the daily routines of all the British. They lived and breathed its direct effects. As one Marlborough war bride remembered, "Our daily lives were governed and controlled by food rationing, clothing coupons, travel restrictions, inconveniences too trivial and many to mention, blackouts, air raid precautions, assigned spare time duties such as fire watching, our lives played out against the ever present dangers of air attack and invasion. Willy-nilly everyone was totally absorbed in the war effort."[56]

The American GI overseas was experiencing the same sense of anonymity that the upheavals in British society had created for British civilians. The American soldier felt a certain degree of freedom in conjunction with this anonymity, a kind of detachment.[57] Added to this was the feeling of immediacy or uncertainty engendered by the course of war. As one anonymous GI commented, "I don't think you English ought to put so much blame on our boys for being wild. Of course we're wild. A lot of us are three or four thousand miles from home, away for the first time, it's the chance of our lives."[58] In addition, as the young, adventuresome GIs were landing in Britain, the British Tommies were leaving in droves. Fifty-two percent of British men between the ages of nineteen and forty had served in the armed forces by 1944, with the majority posted overseas at some point.[59] This fateful combination of GI invasion and Tommy evacuation, added to the new freedom of movement for British women, produced an unprecedented social situation. The American GI happened to be present at a time of heightened emotions and tensions associated with the war and the equally important biological state of early adulthood.

British women who married foreigners usually made their decision during the war while facing upheavals in British society and an uncertain future. There were more working women, more unwed mothers, and more divorces. The general public accepted these events at a time when possible death and injury were far more immediate concerns. The war did provide an atmosphere that allowed young British women to lead their early adult lives in a manner far less restrictive than it would have been otherwise. The women also came into contact with a group of men, the American GIs, whom they would not have met had it not been for the war. But the war also created barriers to marriages between GIs and British women that the couples had to overcome. Hence, these overseas marriages occurred despite the war, not because of it.

3

Overseas Marriages

He would have liked to have been married before D-Day but you had to go through your superior officer, and his commanding officer was not going to let any of his men marry an English girl, period. So you just put in the application and that was it; it didn't go anywhere. You just did not have any other avenue open except to get the girl pregnant. Believe me, some of them did that deliberately.

—Rosa Ebsary

British war brides became immigrants to America by virtue of their marriages to American citizens. These marriages occurred, for the most part, in Great Britain during the war. However, authorities from both the United States and British governments attempted to discourage and sometimes even stop the marriages of these women and American servicemen. The issue of wartime marriages required that officials carefully balance individuals' civil liberties and governments' wartime priorities. The American military was concerned about marriage-related "distractions" such as allotments, insurance, and domestic arrangements. The army, in particular, saw these marriages as complications. Hence, the army eventually would help a GI who wanted sex by providing condoms and medical treatment, but the military hindered relational commitments; it recognized the human urge for fraternization but not for lasting partnership. The result of this policy often meant that British women who dated GIs were suspect and their reputations called into question. However, the couples persevered in the face of opposition; by insisting on marriage they forced the authorities to change their policies.

Although the high incidence of overseas marriages was unique to World War II, the question of marriage between American servicemen and women of foreign nationality was not. In 1918, soon after

American troops began to arrive in Europe, the American Expeditionary Force (AEF) command received requests from American servicemen for permission to marry French women. United States Army officials did not approve of these unions. The War Department and the army recognized the need to safeguard the civil liberties and rights of American citizens so they did not officially deny men the right to marry. Naturally, the United States military believed the main concern of army personnel should be the conduct of the war with Germany. It did not want soldiers to pursue personal matters.

The AEF soldiers, however, refused to comply and demanded a clear statement of rules governing marriage. Eventually the military decided to follow a policy whereby "headquarters declined to give express consent to marriage or to refuse the same."[1] The United States Army's method of discouraging marriage was to ignore the problem. Hence, the issue of marriage between American soldiers and French women fell to the French government. French civil law aided the American army's attempt to stop marriages. The French government required couples to have wedding banns read in the groom's hometown, creating an obvious problem for American soldiers. However, the United States Army did aid soldiers when the French government insisted that Americans prove they were not already married. A statement from a commanding officer that a soldier's affidavit declaring his single status was true, to the best of the army's knowledge, accompanied applications. This requirement brought the United States Army into the process, albeit reluctantly.

Commanding officers of the American Expeditionary Force in World War I had various objections to overseas marriage. One colonel of a cavalry unit noted, "When Pvt W asked permission to marry I refused, as I did in other cases, on the grounds that this was no time to be undertaking new responsibilities and obligations; that we were over here to fight when the time came; and to spend the rest of the time getting ready for it and not to marry and raise families. If Pvt W is allowed to marry this girl it will lead to a number of other cases just exactly like this. I have been through the whole thing twice before in Cuba and the Philippines."[2] The colonel's objections indicate that the army had experienced similar problems with reconciling the inhumanity of war and the urges of human nature at least as far back as the Spanish-American War.

There is little record of the war bride issue in any war, but the limited information about this topic vis-à-vis World War I does provide some basis of comparison with the situation in World War II. Officers of the American Expeditionary Force in the Great War voiced

many of the same concerns and tried to discourage marriages in
much the same way as commanders of the United States Army of
World War II. During World War I, army officials hoped that by pointing out potential problems they could stop soldiers from developing
relationships with foreign women. The officials suggested that commanding officers let their men know that marriage did not confer
special privileges on the foreign-born wife of a serviceman and that
women of dubious character might prey on men for the express
purpose of financial gain in the form of allotments and insurance.
However, the army agreed that instances of pregnancy did warrant
expediting marriages between soldiers and the women "in trouble,"
as happened in World War II. World War I army officials raised similar objections concerning women in the nurses' corps and the Red
Cross, with the added stipulation that they would discharge any woman in these two services who did contract a marriage and would return them to the United States. In March 1919 the military authorities estimated that "several thousand" marriages had taken place
between American soldiers and foreign women.[3]

The point of comparison between World War I and World War II,
however, is limited where marriage is concerned. Far fewer Americans served overseas in World War I compared to World War II and
they served for a much shorter time. While marriage between young
American soldiers and women overseas was not unknown before the
1940s, the global nature of the conflict in the Second World War, the
sizes of the armies involved, the length of service, and the numbers
of troops sent overseas provide a better basis for an examination of
war brides. A good place to begin an investigation is with the Chaplain Corps, whose mandate included the performance of all ecclesi-
astical duties as well as providing guidance and counseling to soldiers
in a variety of personal areas. Marriage and fraternization were two
of the issues chaplains confronted in their capacity as moral arbiters.
The chaplains' role in the marriage of servicemen included discussing the seriousness of the married state with the GIs and prospective
brides to determine their understanding of the responsibilities of
marriage and, on some occasions, coming to conclusions about the
desirability of permitting a particular marriage to take place.

In 1939, in anticipation of the buildup of the armed forces, the
army changed its regulations regarding the duties of the Chaplain
Corps. Henceforth, chaplains could no longer conduct marriages for
enlisted men below grade three without specific written permission
of the army. In 1940, the army extended its restrictions and insisted
that it would not reenlist men who married without obtaining writ-

ten consent. At the same time, servicemen could no longer be court-martialed for failure "to take prophylactic treatment after illicit sexual intercourse," contracting a venereal disease, or "having thus incapacitated themselves for duty." The army, in other words, condoned sex but not marriage.[4] Since the moral well-being of troops fell within the range of duties for the Chaplain Corps, the chaplains shouldered much of the burden of dealing with sexual issues.

Army chaplains' work involving wartime marriage took place at bases within the United States as well as overseas. The number of marriages increased within the States in the early years of the war. Hence, chaplains at various training bases and army posts devoted much of their time to the issue of matrimony. The substantial increase in numbers of marriages worried many officials concerned about hasty courtships and the uncertainty of wartime. This concern over the moral welfare of soldiers dictated much of the work of army chaplains in World War II. The Chaplain Corps's determination to protect men from the "evils" of pre- and/or extramarital sexual relations often pitted them against other branches of the United States Army. Many chaplains expressed concern over the lack of moral standards in the army and complained of the "army's blind eye" policy regarding questions of sex. They noted that the army did nothing to close off-base houses of prostitution in some overseas areas. Some chaplains charged that the army, by participating in regulating local bordellos, contributed to the moral decline of the men. In addition, the provision of condoms to servicemen as they left bases and the establishment of prophylactic stations for their use upon return allegedly acted to encourage immoral behavior. In one chaplain's opinion, the profusion of dirty pictures in servicemen's publications and the display of erotic art on airplanes, as well as profane language and jokes, led to a decline in moral conduct. These issues made the chaplain's job of moral guardian more difficult.[5]

Army rules and regulations concerning marriage and fraternization also made a chaplain's job more complex. In May 1942, just four months after the arrival of the first American troops in Great Britain, a chaplain in Northern Ireland requested clarification of army policy regarding overseas marriages. The army responded by sending him a list of the major drawbacks regarding overseas marriage. Marriage to an American citizen did not automatically give the foreign-born wife United States citizenship. This represented a change in immigration policy since the First World War. United States citizenship now required a three-year residency within the United States of the foreign-born wife. The army also pointed out to the chaplain that marriage did not mean that the soldier could live off-base while overseas. Echoing World War I concerns, the judge advocate noted that a soldier could be moved at any time and "the girl who marries a soldier may reasonably expect to be 'left behind' at any moment, . . . and it would be unwise to become dependent upon the soldier for support."[6] The army also warned the chaplain that he should investigate carefully a soldier's current marital status to avoid the problem of bigamy, which, if it occurred, would mean the foreign wife would have no rights at all. In addition, though marriage would help the foreign-born wife in terms of immigration to the United States, actual transportation to America would be difficult at best and she could not expect to accompany her husband on his return home after the war.

The army often reiterated these points in its correspondence to chaplains relating to soldiers' marriages. As in World War I, the United States Army in the Second World War viewed marriage in general, and overseas marriage in particular, as undesirable. The military was far more concerned with waging war and, reasonably, saw the marriages of its men as a distraction from its primary objectives. Hence, authorities continued to do as much as they could, without directly violating the soldiers' civil liberties, to discourage couples from marrying. War Department circulars and army regulations concerning marriage stressed these points. The army required any soldier contemplating marriage to obtain his commanding officer's permission. At first the army tried to impose a three-month waiting period but later reduced this to two months. Commanding officers could waive the waiting period at their own discretion, which left some flexibility for cases of illegitimacy and pregnancy. The army stressed two additional points on the subject of overseas marriages. First, it was important for the soldier to comply with all civil requirements in the country where the marriage was to take place. Failure to do so could result in an invalid marriage. Second, the army still held out against any marriage that would appear to bring discredit to the military. Although the army mentioned the last point frequently, it never clearly defined what it meant by discredit. The army obviously wanted to retain control over soldiers' marriage plans.[7]

Other Chaplain Corps duties entailed dealing with the outside publicity generated by the news of overseas marriages. In 1942, Chief of Chaplains Major General William Arnold heard from a very unhappy woman in Sioux City, Iowa. She stated that she believed the best course of action for the army to take regarding overseas marriages would be to ban them. Due to the length of the war and the time soldiers would spend overseas, the vast numbers of American soldiers in the service, and the anticipated high casualty rate, she reasoned that America would be short of men of marrying age at the end of the war. This problem would result in numerous instances of American girls who would lead lonely and unfulfilled lives in direct consequence of the army policy of allowing soldiers to marry foreign-born women. The woman pointed out that "already thousands of American girls know they face spinsterhood and a life of loneliness and unhappiness. . . . To allow Americans to marry Irish, English, Australian and Icelandic girls during all the years the war may last will be tragic for American girls."[8] She noted that recent publicity often stressed the opportunity these marriages provided for the United States and other countries to become closer allies. From her point of view, however, the moral and social ramifications, as well as the simple distress of American girls, were not worth the sacrifice. She predicted that "a war of five years or even less will mean hundreds of thousands of such marriages."[9]

The Chief of Chaplains Assistant responded to the woman's letter by suggesting that his office was "of the opinion that relatively few American soldiers will marry foreign girls" and that press reports were exaggerating the few cases that had occurred by May 1942. He assured her that her fears were "needless since the number who will marry foreign girls . . . will be practically negligible." He also commented that since the Chaplain Corps was well represented throughout the army, the soldiers who did contemplate overseas marriage would be subject to influence from chaplains who "will counsel and advise the soldiers accordingly."[10]

The exchange between the woman in Iowa and the Chief of Chaplains Assistant serves as an excellent example of civilian concern over overseas marriages and the power of the press in publicizing this phenomenon. The first marriages received attention from various news sources including the soldiers' magazine *Yank* and newspaper *Stars and Stripes*. Opposition within the United States to overseas marriages sometimes bordered on the hysterical. United States congress members received hundreds of letters from irate citizens concerning the practice of allowing American soldiers to marry foreign women while overseas. Press accounts when the war brides arrived in the United States made a point of stressing how wrong the American public had been previously to object to the marriages. Fear that foreign women were taking advantage of GIs was the basis of most complaints.

The question of overseas marriages caused concern among the chaplains themselves. Chaplain Captain Charles Dever recorded his own reaction to the subject of wartime marriages in response to a questionnaire to chaplains on the subject of marriage. Captain Dever noted that in general he approved "of the marriages in the sense that the soldiers have something more or less tangible to steady their lives and therefore make better soldiers. However, many of them are marriages that come as a result of the uniform and the stress of the times."[11] A number of chaplains in overseas stations shared Captain Dever's concerns. Some chaplains faced the problem of trying to reconcile army policy with their own moral standards and religious functions. In 1943 a chaplain stationed in Iceland wrote to the Chief of Chaplains office to complain about army policy forbidding American soldiers serving in Iceland to marry. He noted that while the army provided condoms and prophylactic stations for men who went out on pass, "the man who came from America, unmarried and not engaged, and who wanted to remain decent and get married could not do so." The chaplain was unable to offer any comfort to soldiers who came to him for help and advice. The problem was especially acute because army policy meant there were approximately two hundred illegitimate children in Iceland. The chaplain suggested that this was "a policy encouraging bastardy."[12]

The response of the Chief of Chaplains office was typical of army policy on these issues: the problem of overseas marriages should be left to the local army authority of each region. The Chief of Chaplains office noted that there had even been a recent conference on the subject of overseas marriage that had concluded that the best course of action was to counsel delay. In the specific case of illegitimate births, the army authorities counseled the chaplain to let men know that they could have allotments deducted from their pay for children they wished to acknowledge. The Chief of Chaplains response did not address the deeper moral question that the chaplain's letter had highlighted. Instead, the chaplain in Iceland was reprimanded with an admonition "that chaplains devote themselves to advising those under their moral and religious care to be long suffering and patient in the midst of difficulties and to work, hope and pray for a victory that will make for a world where freedom really exists and its fruits may be enjoyed. The chaplains by their good example and hopeful attitude can add a mighty stimulus toward the prosecution of the war and ultimate victory. When chaplains are short-sighted, growlers and easily discouraged, the way becomes dark indeed."[13] Like the rest of army policy relating to moral and religious issues, this advice offered no real solution and clearly put the conduct of the war above moral considerations as well as the physical and emotional welfare of soldiers, women, and children.

To their credit, the army and the War Department were equally reluctant to become involved in requests for firmer prohibitions of marriage or a more restrictive approach to moral issues. The previously cited examples of chaplains' complaints concerning the army attitude toward prostitution and the encouragement of prophylactic treatment are cases in point. Additionally, other chaplains took exception to the army policy of allowing marriages at all. One chaplain submitted a report to his superiors suggesting that the army should discourage wartime marriages at all costs. Of paramount importance to this chaplain was not the moral issue of men's souls but rather the more prosaic consideration of their wallets. He believed that the majority of women contracting overseas marriages were doing so for the express purpose of cheating the government out of allotments and benefits. He stated that it was outrageous that foreign women "who have never been in the country, born [sic] its tax burden, or shared its cross of war" could profit from marrying an American. He went on to suggest that "the lure of American gold, freedom, and glamor lowers the bars. Most AWOLs are tracable [sic] to sex affairs: but, American men are too galant [sic], honorable, and yet emotional in foreign lands to make sound decisions in marriage matters. More red tape should be added to make marriage harder and harder to win."[14]

The War Department's response to this complaint was typical of the hands-off approach mentioned earlier. Policies and regulations on overseas marriages consistently followed a pattern of first attempting to discourage and then sitting back and allowing nature to take its course. The army decision-making process during World War II on this particular issue proves that policy did not dictate actions but rather followed events. When American GIs first began seeking permission to marry foreign-born women, the army tried to prohibit the marriages; and when the GIs insisted on pursuing their civil liberties concerning moral questions (both marriage and sexual relations), the army policy then began to play a game of catching up with the soldier. As a result, military authorities issued circular after circular, and each new regulation or policy was a belated attempt to deal with a fait accompli. For example, wartime marriages had been grounds to refuse reenlistment earlier but, when this failed to stop marriages, the regulation changed. The army then insisted on a three-month waiting period and the commanding officer's approval. The waiting period later changed to two months with the possibility of having the period waived. The army, at one time, dismissed American soldiers of World War II for contracting a venereal disease but later provided them with condoms and pro-stations. The military could not regulate social behavior despite repeated attempts. It could not control GI conduct no matter which approach it adopted.

The American Red Cross, an institution purportedly responsible for soldiers' welfare and morale, also became involved in the issue of overseas marriage. Red Cross participation included the controversial area of marriage investigations. Early in the war, military authorities asked the Red Cross to conduct investigations into the backgrounds of potential GI brides. Red Cross representatives visited the homes of the women and subsequently submitted reports on their family circumstances. When news of these inquiries spread into the public domain, a furor arose. The Red Cross was accused of conducting character investigations. As a result of this negative publicity, the American Red Cross subsequently changed its policy and removed itself from the practice of marriage investigations. From the organization's point of view, "Those advocating Red Cross participation noted the aftermath of the last war when the hasty Franco-American marriages resulted in many tragedies and much unhappiness. If American soldiers and the French girls had been properly advised probably a great many of these domestic misfortunes would have been avoided."[15]

The American Red Cross took a very paternalistic approach to discouraging overseas marriage, in much the same way as had the United States Army. In addition, the American Red Cross (like the army) believed that it was capable of determining what constituted adequate foundations for a marriage, an assumption that begs for argument. The army and the American Red Cross seemed to assume that couples contracting overseas marriages were not doing so out of love but rather for some hidden reason that, once discovered, could be brought to light, thus stopping the process. The participants in question were usually consenting adults but the agencies involved felt it was their responsibility to pass judgment on these marriages. Even if one concedes that the army's concern for keeping all military personnel focused on the conduct of the war was legitimate, this paternalistic approach raises some interesting ethical questions.

From late 1943 onward, after withdrawing from marriage investigations, the American Red Cross took responsibility only in providing information to the soldier and his bride on military regulations governing marriage. It also acted as a clearinghouse for soldiers interested in obtaining information on the legal ramifications of international marriage and counseled servicemen and their war brides on

United States government policies concerning immigration and citizenship. The American Red Cross followed its more traditional role of catering to soldiers' welfare by keeping servicemen informed of the rights of dependents to military allotments, giving monetary aid when necessary, and helping soldiers to verify birth certificates and other legal documents. After marriages had occurred, the Red Cross provided counseling to war brides on the nature of American society and culture. All of this was available to the American soldiers and war brides on a voluntary basis.[16] The American Red Cross followed the same procedures in most overseas theaters.

The attitude of numerous agencies toward overseas marriages had various effects on the women involved. Potential war brides had to confront resistance to their plans at every turn. They were the victims of the pervasive idea that somehow they were suspect. The marriage investigations were just one procedure that threw doubt on the morals and character of any foreign woman who met and married an American soldier. A reputation for being fast and loose followed many of these women from the time they were dating the GIs until after they landed in the United States. As Joan Posthuma recalled of her own experience, "I went up to get my papers [and] I got this very snooty girl. You had to have your marriage certificate and your birth certificate and everything and I handed them in and she looked at it and she said, 'What were you doing, waiting on the dock for the first Yank to get off the boat?'"[17] Ivy Hammers blamed the military: "I resent the way the U.S. Army treated some of the girls. Some of them were treated like dirt, as if they were asking for the moon."[18]

The women's native governments also dealt with the problems of international marriage. Since British servicemen met and married women of other nationalities while serving overseas, the British government had to address the question of overseas marriages from both sides. The Foreign Office played a major role in handling British officials' concerns about these international marriages. The Air Ministry gathered considerable information from various allied legal staffs about the legal rights of British women who married foreigners. The ministry drew up an outline of the consequences of marriage of British women to allied soldiers, including those from America, Belgium, Czechoslovakia, Holland, France, Norway, and Poland. This information was for use by British officials when counseling women about marriage to foreigners. The British government was less concerned over the legal status of the considerable number of British women who married soldiers from commonwealth nations such as Canada, Australia, South Africa, and New Zealand.[19]

The most important issue in the view of the British government was the woman's citizenship upon marriage. For the British war bride who married a Dutch, Czechoslovakian, Belgian, Norwegian, or Polish serviceman, marriage led to automatic citizenship in her husband's country with a consequent loss of British citizenship. The British woman who married a Frenchman could declare herself a French citizen and at the same time retain her British citizenship. Marriage to an American, as the United States military authorities had pointed out in directives on numerous occasions, did not automatically give American citizenship to the spouse. Immigrants to America could obtain citizenship only through application for naturalization after a period of residency in the United States. The United States government reduced the period of residency for war brides from five to three years.

The Air Ministry's summary of rights did not mention the status of the woman's British citizenship upon marriage to an American. The British government eventually allowed dual citizenship as long as women did not formally renounce their British citizenship. For the war brides this meant potential future access to health and pension services in Britain.[20] The ministry also provided considerable additional information on the nature of interracial marriages between British women and black American soldiers. The British government reiterated a point that the American military had frequently noted, namely that "a marriage which is against the law of any state of domicile of either party . . . will be invalid everywhere." The ministry went on to explain that interracial marriages fell within this category in parts of the United States where "such marriages are . . . regarded as odious."[21]

A further complication pertained to the status of children born of British women and men of the allied forces. The concern here was whether such children born in Britain were automatic citizens of their father's country. For each of the allied nations on the ministry's list, children in these international marriages acquired citizenship from both the parents' countries, until adulthood.

The British government's disquiet over the legal ramifications of these marriages was understandable. If, for some reason, problems developed in areas of citizenship and the validity of marriage, British women needed to understand their rights. For example, Australian women who married Americans automatically lost their citizenship upon marriage but did not receive American citizenship. Consequently, Australian war brides were stateless. The issue of citizenship became even more important as the war ended and women began the process of being reunited with their husbands.

   The British government's concern about the rights of its female subjects was understandable also in the face of the attitude of American officials. The American military had made it very clear that it was not happy about the romantic liaisons that its servicemen developed in Britain during the war. The British government was equally doubtful about these marriages. Whereas the American government feared the marriages were a distraction to the war effort and an attempt by British gold-diggers to get either American money or entry to the United States, the British government worried that American servicemen were deceiving part of its citizenry and taking advantage of women during unstable wartime conditions. Regardless of all these objections by United States and British authorities, wartime marriages occurred regularly.

   The two United States armed forces' publications, *Yank* and *Stars and Stripes,* carried articles and letters about overseas marriages and military regulations throughout the war. In a July 1942 article in *Yank* the headline, "Don't Promise Her Anything—Marriage Outside the U.S. Is Out," overstated the situation. The article, however, noted that marriage to a foreign woman was possible but required a commanding officer's permission. The article also warned that "Washington sources are inclined to doubt that commanding officers of expeditionary forces will approve marital ventures except in rare cases." The Washington, D.C., authorities counseled against marriages due to the potential conflict between agencies on issues such as immigration and the "sudden and frequent movement of troops."[22]

   Yank and *Stars and Stripes* also served as forums for GI questions about overseas marriages and subsequent problems. Several GIs wrote to ask if their wives would have to wait to gain entry to the United States as part of the immigration quota for Britain. The advice column let them know that foreign-born wives of American servicemen could enter the United States as nonquota immigrants. Other GIs asked how to get a furlough from Europe to go back to England to marry, inquired whether a marriage conducted without a commanding officer's permission was valid, and sought to learn what the citizenship status of war brides would be. These publications also reported stories about the first marriages in some theaters of operation, problems of GIs rotated home who were unable to get their fiancées into the United States to get married, and the status of dependency allotments after marriage. The volume of stories in the pages of *Yank* and *Stars and Stripes* illustrates the frequency of these wartime weddings. One reporter noted that of the original one hundred single members of a United States unit in Northern Ireland, fifty were en-

gaged or already married to Irish and English women within a year
of the unit's arrival.[23]

On the one hand the United States military saw these marriages
as "a passing fad with post-war complications" and tried to discourage them.[24] On the other side British authorities wanted the American military to "exercise increased caution" when granting permission for soldiers to wed.[25] The men and women involved were caught
in the middle. One former GI, Ted Hammers, remembered hearing
about "a lot of fellows. They wouldn't okay them to get married. Lots
of them. They figured it was just a fling and they would be sorry."[26]
Rosa Ebsary recalled that families also tried to discourage marriages. Speaking of her own case, she said that her brothers "went and
told everybody about it. I remember one of my sister's former boy-
friends saying, 'Et tu, Brute?' I really must say that everybody liked
Edwin but they weren't really crazy about the idea."[27] June Porter, a
younger war bride, recalled the resistance of her family when she
"had a letter that asked me to marry him, he wanted to get engaged.
. . . My mother said, 'No way.' I was then seventeen going on eighteen . . . and she had married when she was seventeen. Of course I
was obviously throwing it up at her. I said, 'Well, you got married.' I
begged for a week. My mother and father said, 'No way. You can't go
all that way, you're too young.' At the end of the week I had broken
them down. One week."[28]

Perhaps the worst part of this resistance was the sense of isolation it created. It took fortitude for many brides and husbands to
overcome all the objections. The sense of frustration prompted Sybil
Afdem to reflect that "you had some horrendous tales from everybody. I honestly can't think of one person that I knew that said,
'Good for you, go and get it.' Not one. They all knew tales of people who got over there and they were left there with nothing or they
had got over there and there was nobody to meet them and nowhere to go. They never told you of anybody who went over there
and was happy. . . . We didn't have that much family, really, but everybody, all our family, all our friends, they did everything to dis-
suade me from coming."[29]

While British and American authorities and civilians on both sides
of the Atlantic voiced anxiety over the motivations behind marriages, the GIs and British women had a wholly different opinion. Their
marriages were not the result of grand designs or dictated by any
ulterior motives. Many women resented being questioned about their
reasons for marrying. Rosa Ebsary pointed out that she was "twenty-
one and Ed was twenty-four. This was not an overnight deal. . . . I

The wedding party of Corporal Florence Hutson, Women's Auxiliary Air Force, and Corporal Edward A. Steager, United States Army, 22 December 1944, London. (Courtesy Barbara Steager Malone)

Rainbow Corner, operated by the American Red Cross in London, offered instruction and assistance to the war brides. (Press Association Picture Library, London)

War brides gathered on the deck of the *Queen Mary,* en route to America, March 1946. (Press Association Picture Library, London)

Taking the air aboard the *Queen Mary,* March 1946. (Press Association Picture Library, London)

Mothers and their babies shared quarters with other war brides onboard ship. (Press Association Picture Library, London)

War brides salute the Statue of Liberty as the *Queen Mary* prepares to dock at New York Harbor, March 1946. (Queen Mary Seaport Photo)

Ted and Ivy (Barnes) Hammers
on their wedding day, 24 July
1946, Detroit, Michigan. (Courtesy Ted and Ivy Hammers)

A group of British war brides from throughout the United States met for
a reunion at Bolton, Lancashire, England, in September 1993. (Courtesy
Pat Morgan, Transatlantic Brides and Parents Association)

hadn't gone haring and scaring around the country. Ed and I wrote every day to each other, I still have a trunk full of letters."[30] For many women the decision to marry an American was the same as the decision to marry anyone; it was based on strong emotion. Sybil Afdem confessed that her husband was "all I could see. He was my life, my whole life, always, even to the day he died."[31]

Servicemen also resented the obstacles to and innuendoes about wartime marriages. One GI in Northern Ireland, responding to comments made by a Washington, D.C., official against overseas marriages in the pages of *Yank,* pointed out that military regulations governing marriages were so complex and lengthy that these marriages were not hasty or ill-conceived. The GI noted that American servicemen did not need somebody suggesting the United States government should make marriage even more difficult to conclude. There was already, in his opinion, enough red tape in place. He asked the official if "it ever occur[red] to you, sir, that we who have married over here could be in love with our wives just as much as we would be if they were American? Or that for many of us, 'the girl who married dear old dad' may have been a 'foreigner' too?"[32]

To the British war brides and American GIs the issue of overseas marriage had little to do with military regulations or social issues; it was simply a case of meeting someone, falling in love, and getting married. While the war and the authorities did have an impact on these relationships, it was, more important, a case of young couples who came together at marriageable age, when they would have been meeting people of the opposite sex, courting, and getting married had they stayed at home and had there been no war. Undoubtedly the war did temporarily free up the morals of British society, but the data used to support this thesis—i.e., a rise in venereal disease and illegitimacy rates—do not translate to the issue of marriage.

The ages of the men and women when they met and married help to explain the phenomenon of war brides. The former American GIs in the 1989 survey were, on average, twenty-five when they got married; the war brides, twenty-one. They were a uniformly young segment of society. Having met and married in large numbers in Britain during the war, once the war was over British war brides faced the consequences of marriage to a foreigner. The majority of British women may have grown up with the expectation of marriage and motherhood but certainly not marriage to anyone other than a countryman. Many of these women had children after marriage but before they lived with their husbands as man and wife. Their courtships had been unusual due to the war, and the war and their different nationalities also made their marriage situations unique. Once married, the couples did not quietly "settle down." War brides' marriages to Americans meant immigration, a prospect that few British women had entertained before meeting their GI husbands.

4

Gaining Entry to America

I wrote to her and started getting all the papers ready
to get her over here. I had a pack of papers. You would
be surprised what they wanted, they wanted everything
under the sun about you: how much money you had,
your whole life, practically, on paper in order to get her
over here.

—Ted Hammers

Once married to GIs, the British war brides faced the prospect of immigration to America. Unfortunately, United States legislation and
army policy in the early days of the war did not make immigration or
transportation easy for the newlyweds. Most of the women fell outside
of the existing army transportation network by virtue of their marriages
to men in the lower grades of the services. In addition, while the war
brides could enter the United States as wives of citizens, existing legislation still required them to have visas and could entail possible rejec-
tion. However, the sheer number of World War II war brides, 115,000
in all, put pressure on authorities to make changes in policy.[1] The United States military eventually had to rewrite its regulations governing
transportation to address the issue of the large number of marriages
contracted by servicemen in the lower ranks. In addition, faced with
the prospect of over 100,000 new immigrants who were married to U.S.
citizens, the American government had to enact special legislation to
govern their entry outside of the existing immigration process. Hence,
gaining entry to America for British war brides involved two interrelated issues: transportation and immigration.

At the outbreak of World War II, United States Army regulations
provided for transportation of wives and dependents of American
servicemen who were officers or enlisted men of the first three grades.
The lowest four grades were not eligible to receive government as-

sisted travel for their families. In addition, since September 1922, foreign women who married United States citizens no longer automatically received American citizenship but had to go through the same naturalization process as any other immigrants. Wives (but not husbands) of American service personnel could enter the United States as nonquota immigrants although they did need to obtain a visa for entry into the United States. Some foreign-born spouses were ineligible for entrance into the United States if they were of a race that was not eligible for future citizenship "such as, East Indians, natives of Southeastern Asia and islands of the Southwest Pacific area."[2] Their entrance into the United States would require special consideration from immigration authorities.

Interestingly, the transport issue arose before the immigration policy changed. By late 1943 the United States Army, War and State Departments, and other government and private agencies such as the Red Cross confronted the problem of war bride transportation. The concern of the American Red Cross was that the financial burden of dependent travel would fall to it in its capacity of providing assistance to families of service personnel. Government authorities had no clear plan to cover the transportation of foreign-born dependents from overseas. This had not been a large problem in World War I when immigration restrictions had been minimal and the number of overseas brides was relatively small. By the midpoint of World War II various agencies set up a committee to investigate the potential problems associated with war bride transportation. The committee wanted to review the legal basis of war bride immigration and to make sure that the new immigrants would not become financial burdens to the United States.[3] By 1943 the American Red Cross was receiving requests from GIs for financial assistance in bringing their wives to the United States, especially servicemen in the four lowest grades whose dependents were not eligible for free government transportation. The American Red Cross declined to provide financial assistance but did agree to help servicemen's wives in other ways such as filling out forms. In 1944 army transportation policy changed to include dependents of servicemen of all grades. Faced with demands for help from thousands of GIs who had contracted marriages, the majority of whom were in the lowest ranks, the United States military had little choice but to alter its policy. While the issue of who would receive transport was decided, wives and children still had to obtain visas for immigration to the United States.[4]

Both the American soldier and the British bride had to complete numerous forms for the wife to obtain a visa. The soldier petitioned

Immigration and Naturalization Services for his wife's entry into the United States and included copies of his own birth certificate or naturalization papers, divorce or spouse's death certification if previously married, proof of pay and allotment, list of dependents, bank account verification, and employer affidavit in his submission to authorities. If the Immigration Service approved the husband's petition, then the American consul nearest the woman's home notified her of her approved status and she then had to apply in person for the visa. The regulations required that war brides would provide proof of sufficient funds to finance the trip, a passport, birth certificate, marriage certificate, proof of divorce or spouse's death if previously married, service record if previously in armed forces, medical certificate, exit permit, and evidence that transportation would be available within a specific time after the date of visa application (usually four months).[5]

The United States government admitted children of marriages between American servicemen and foreign-born women without restriction and without need to apply for nonquota status since they were automatically American citizens as long as their fathers were "over 21 at the time of the child's birth and [had] lived in the United States for 10 years, 5 of which, including service in the U.S. forces abroad, were after his sixteenth birthday."[6] Children from previous marriages or illegitimate children who were not the offspring of an American citizen had to enter the United States as part of the quota for their country. This meant that step-children of GIs had to apply for immigration under the existing quota laws.

Once a war bride had her visa she could request transportation. Typical bureaucratic nightmares ensued for some war brides. Ivy Hammers recalled her own frustration:

I started by going to different British places for my passport. . . . I spent hours in line at these different organizations in Westminster. I would start out early in the morning and go all day through these offices. In those days you had to have a visa, but you couldn't get your visa without a passport and you couldn't get your passport without a visa. My birthday was 2 July and I was at the passport office and the official there had promised me my passport and it wasn't there. I just broke down in tears right over his desk and in no time I was in another place to get a paper and the girl said, "You will get this in about six months." I couldn't believe it. How was I going to live for six months? I had no job, nothing. I had to pay rent where I was, I didn't know what was going to happen. So she looked down at my papers and she said, "You were born in Cardiff. So was I. Come back tomorrow." I got my papers in about twenty days, which was unheard of. Six, seven months would be nothing, it would be good.[7]

Having obtained a visa, war brides submitting applications for transportation faced another lengthy paper trail. Women needed to send a copy of a permission-to-leave certificate from their own government and an application for transportation to her husband's commanding officer. The serviceman needed to fill in the application or, if he was unavailable, the United States Army required proof that the serviceman wanted his dependent to receive transportation to America. The U.S. government requirement that GIs fill out forms was a method of ensuring that those wives no longer wanted by their GI husbands as well as women illicitly using the war bride system as a means to gain entry into the United States did not receive transportation. Once war brides completed the paperwork, the United States government put them on a transportation waiting list. War bride transportation was at a minimum while the war was still in progress since army policy gave priority in shipping to wounded servicemen, ex-prisoners of war, men being redeployed, or those few who were eligible for discharge. Women could book passage with commercial firms but this type of transportation was in short supply and the cost was prohibitive for many.

Women of foreign birth engaged to American servicemen encountered the biggest hurdles when they wanted to travel to the United States to wed. Fiancées of GIs had to enter the country as quota emigrants from their respective countries. This presented a major problem for women who lived in areas of small quota numbers. The British quota was large and was never a factor for these war brides, but for other countries the American Red Cross estimated that "for a fiancee to come in on a regular quota visa might delay entry into the U.S. for 20 years in some instances." In the war years the United States Army did not make any special arrangements for fiancées of American servicemen, and neither did the American Red Cross. Both agencies believed that the question of fiancée immigration was best "left to the post war period."[8]

One possibility open to fiancées was to apply to United States authorities for a visitor's visa. Under this plan the fiancée would arrive in the United States, get married, and then leave the United States and apply for reentry as a nonquota immigrant wife of a United States serviceman. Women who followed this course could potentially mar-

ry in the United States and then retreat to Canada to await entry. This
was an option open more to women from countries in the British
Commonwealth such as Britain and Australia and those with enough
money to sustain themselves through the whole process. Part of the
problem with this method was that local American consuls could deny
the applicant if they believed the purpose of the visit was to marry
an American. Denial of an application had much to do with officials'
concerns that women who skirted regular procedures for overseas
marriage and immigration were likely to become public charges if the
marriage did not take place. War bride applicants needed a statement
from the American serviceman or his family that they would provide
for her maintenance and that she would not become a burden to the
state. No one vouched for fiancées on visitor's visas but they did have
to have a considerable amount of money to initiate this process. In
some cases the Immigration and Naturalization Service required visitors to post a departure bond and, in most cases, "have funds for
necessary travel and maintenance."[9]

The army command adamantly refused to consider the issue of
fiancée immigration, believing that its only concern was with married
serviceman. This position was consistent with the army's firm policy
of discouraging marriages in the first place. The United States government eventually conceded the necessity for some arrangement for
fiancées of American servicemen by requiring women who applied
for visitor's visas to fulfill part of the war bride application process
for permanent entry into the United States, such as providing proof
of future support, to avoid becoming dependent on United States
government social services. The State Department and the Immigration Service made special arrangements for women from countries
with small quota numbers including "Australia, New Zealand, Spain,
Portugal, and Greece . . . if certain conditions are met," such as supplying the statement of support.[10] This arrangement also covered the
foreign-born women's children from previous marriages.

The issues of immigration and transportation of foreign-born wives
and fiancées of American servicemen eventually reached the level of
the Congress of the United States. The number of agencies and departments involved in the process of war bride immigration (i.e.,
Army, Navy, State Department, War Department, Immigration and
Naturalization Service, consuls, embassies), resulted in confusion and
conflicting regulations. Prior to December 1945, immigrant wives of
American citizens entered the United States under provisions of the
1924 immigrant legislation as the wives of United States citizens. On
29 November 1945, Representative Dickstein introduced House Bill

HR4857, which provided for "the admission to the United States of alien spouses and alien minor children of citizen members of the United States armed forces."[11] This act amended the 1917 and 1924 immigration acts and was to be in force for three years from the date of passage. It allowed "alien spouses or alien children of United States citizens serving in, or having an honorable discharge certificate from the armed forces of the United States during the Second World war . . . to be admitted to the United States."[12] The Immigration and Naturalization Service committee unanimously supported passage of the bill. Previous reasons for the exclusion of immigrants, such as physical or mental defects, would not apply to the war brides, but the act still required the medical examination. The committee "estimated there are approximately 75,000 to 100,000 spouses of American service people throughout the world and that approximately 40,000 to 55,000 will come from Great Britain."[13] The War Brides Act did not generate opposition and became Public Law 271 when both houses approved it on 28 December 1945.[14] The immediate effect was to waive the visa and exclusion requirements, as previously mentioned. However, the American serviceman husband, if discharged by this time, had to prove it was an honorable discharge. This piece of legislation did not overturn immigration restrictions on foreign-born spouses who were "racially" ineligible for American citizenship.

In June 1946 the United States Congress passed Public Law 471, which addressed the question of the admission of the "alien fiancee or fiance of a citizen who is serving in, or who has been honorably discharged from the armed forces of the United States during World War II."[15] Persons entering the United States under this act would travel on passport visas as in-transit nonimmigrant visitors. The act was originally in effect for one year and the length of stay restricted to three months. The visitor had to be from a race of people eligible for immigration to the United States and had to provide proof of a sincere intention to marry. The legislation stipulated that "in the event the marriage does not occur within the period for which the alien was admitted, the alien shall be required to depart . . . and upon failure to do so shall be deported."[16] To cover the cost of deportation, the law required that the intended couple post a five hundred dollar bond before entry to the United States. The American Red Cross estimated that this new law would affect 1,500 fiancées in Australia, 15,000 in the United Kingdom, and 1,000 in Europe. The act did not apply to the children of women engaged to American GIs unless they were recognized children of an American citizen. These potential step-children had to apply for a visa under separate arrangements, but the Immigration Services instructed American consuls to give them priority.[17]

Congress had felt compelled to take action in late 1945 for several reasons, including the heavy volume of visa applications at American embassies overseas and the pressures exerted by the couples. Many GIs, recently discharged or redeployed, wrote to their congress members for aid in getting their wives to the United States. Some American husbands even tried to obtain visas from the British embassy so they could return to the United Kingdom. The British government, however, was reluctant to issue visas since housing and other resources were in such short supply. The pressures for United States government action on the British war brides issue continued to build in Britain. By late 1945 the American embassy was averaging 500 visitors a day requesting visa information. The figure was inflated because some of the visitors were repeat applicants and, with the end of the war in Europe, more people were applying. Nonetheless, the American embassy estimated that it received visits from a total of 40,000 war brides between 1942 and 1945. The American embassy in London also recorded over 1,000 letters a day in late 1945. Unfortunately, according to one source, the system had processed only 3,000 British women by early October 1945.

Once the United States government defined who was eligible for transportation and immigration to America, the only thing left to do was find the ships. Unfortunately, the shipping was not available. The army gave priority in shipping to the wounded, former prisoners of war, combat veterans, and men with high "discharge" point totals. Nevertheless, as early as September 1944, *Stars and Stripes* reported the arrival of GI brides in America. A contingent of 295 Australian war brides had arrived in San Francisco accompanied by 74 children. A week later the newspaper reported that 60 war brides and 16 children had arrived in New York from Northern Ireland; the article stated that this was the "first such group" to come to America from the United Kingdom and that the women and children filled empty slots on a United States transport that was shipping navy personnel back to the states.[18] Despite these claims, some war brides had secured travel to America even earlier. These women arrived in the United States before the end of the war in Europe and before the war bride transportation and immigration system was in place. Hence, they do not figure into official statistics. Unfortunately, even though their numbers were small, the publicity surrounding their transportation worked against other war brides. Numerous Americans, both overseas military personnel and civilians at home, resented this use of scarce transportation. Moreover, many of the war brides awaiting transportation viewed these early accounts with a great deal of envy and frustration. From mid- to late 1945 these various opinions clashed on the pages of newspapers and in the streets of London.

GIs often recorded their opinions on transportation of war brides in the pages of the service newspapers. The most frequent suggestion of disgruntled servicemen who were not married to foreign women was that shipping space on military transports be reserved for American servicemen. Several GIs in Australia wanted the government to allocate the space to combat troops who were eligible for rotation. The transportation of war brides was especially galling to men who had applied for transportation and been denied due to lack of space. One private noted that by rights the American GI should come first while another suggested that the United States government should "let the women wait."[19] When newspapers went so far as to devote articles or pictures to the arrival of war brides in the United States, GI complaints grew louder. One corporal suggested that such newspaper stories worked against maintaining morale, especially for ex-POWs like himself or combat wounded recovering in United Kingdom–based army hospitals. The men suggested that the women should wait and that their GI husbands should agree. One infantryman even proposed that his hospital stay, while seeming to be interminable, would not be quite so bad and the use of shipping space by brides a bit more palatable if the United States Army would use the returning trips to bring American women to the United Kingdom.[20]

British war brides, awaiting transportation, reacted in a variety of ways to the long delays. Continuous publicity motivated numerous war brides to become more vocal in their push for transportation. They were feeling increased strain at the delay of travel as the army shipped their husbands out of Europe for potential redeployment or demobilization. By the summer of 1945 these strains and frustrations became apparent. One British bride who wrote to *Stars and Stripes* bemoaning the lack of transportation found that her letter and her moniker ("Disgusted GI Bride") created a furor within the magazine's pages. Several GIs wrote in to suggest that this particular bride was incredibly selfish and misguided since the transportation for all brides that she demanded would displace American GIs who had been away from home for several years. While insisting that the wounded had priority, one group of GIs told "Disgusted" that "another 12 months, we're sure, won't hurt you"; another GI expressed his sympathy for her husband. In the same issue of *Stars and Stripes* that carried GI responses, another war bride wrote in to distance herself and other women from the sentiments of the disgusted wife. She agreed with United States Army priority listing for shipping, which included "combat soldiers who have fought to save England."[21] She acknowledged both her shame at being associated with a war bride like "Disgusted" and her willingness to wait patiently for transportation until all American GIs had returned to the States, however long that might take.

In a counterpoint to these developments, GI husbands of foreign-born women wrote in to give their opinions of the delay in bringing war brides to the United States. The letter writers described the policy of the United States Army as "another indication of the contemptuous and arbitrary treatment [received by] GIs who have married while on foreign service." They complained of being treated like "moral lepers" and reminded those who questioned the right of GI brides to transportation that the women married United States servicemen who deserved to have their families treated with respect. In addition, the GIs commented on the fact that the Canadian authorities seemed to have addressed the problem of transporting war brides without any problems while the American soldier continued to have to battle the United States government's bureaucratic approach to "the domestic problems of their soldiers." Another GI remarked that a West Virginia Congressman counseling delay of war bride transportation was misguided; "I think I'm entitled to that trip for my wife, and I don't think Uncle Sam should stand in the way of my getting her back to America as soon as possible."[22]

In June 1945 the army had announced further delays in the transportation of GI brides, perhaps as long as ten to twelve months, while it focused on an all-out effort to bring the boys home from Europe. Although the army had announced in November 1944 the policy of providing free government transportation for GI dependents overseas, regardless of rank, "personnel with higher priorities" were to receive first shipping space.[23] While some GIs rejoiced as news of the massive movement of troops to America grabbed the headlines, others were reluctant to leave because it meant leaving behind a wife, and sometimes children, to face a difficult situation alone. The lack of any clear indication of when dependent transportation would be available raised serious questions for the couples. How long would it be before they were reunited? If left alone, how could the women face the endless sea of red tape and frequently changing army regulations and policies?

The continuing publication of misinformation about transportation to America did little to ease the minds of the war brides. In July 1945 newspapers in Britain heralded the imminent departure of GI wives from British shores. Misleading headlines declared, "Soldiers' Families Promised Early Passage 'Home,'" while British women waited for official news from United States authorities. The *Daily Express* told British war brides "to be ready to sail in October and November." The newspaper had no qualms about speculating on the reasons for this abrupt change in the war bride transportation saga. Shipping space would be available, according to the staff reporter, because the war with Japan would end sooner than expected and more passenger liners would be available to carry the brides. In addition, the shipment of American troops from Britain was said to be "well ahead of schedule."[24] While speculation occurred in the newspapers, the United States government still had nothing official to say.

In all the publicity surrounding war bride transportation, at least one accurate headline appeared in the pages of *Stars and Stripes*: "Transportation of Foreign Brides Gives Uncle Sam a Headache." In August 1945 the army estimated that fifty thousand British and ten to twenty thousand Australian brides needed transportation. Countering the optimistic pronouncements of the London papers, the army noted that future shipping space might not be available until spring 1946. While "many wives . . . don't like the delay and some are threatening divorce" the army continued to reiterate its commitment to providing transportation eventually but refused to change its policy on the issue of making space available immediately.[25]

The controversy continued to build until it finally erupted in October 1945. The first signs of protest appeared in Bristol where a number of war brides demonstrated their frustration by organizing a baby show as a means of calling attention to their plight.[26] In addition, while Australian war brides and their children landed in San Francisco on the ship *Lurline*, GIs in Australia protested that the war brides had taken space away from American servicemen. At the same time, the United States government finally sent a commission to Great Britain to deal directly with the question of dependent transportation. This commission, organized at the request of the United States ambassador to Britain, left for the United Kingdom in early October to "work out with the Army and the Navy a program which would be just to all concerned," both the brides and the returning servicemen.[27]

October 1945 turned out to be a month of high drama in the British war bride story. A large group of war brides staged a protest in London on the eleventh. Several hundred of them marched to the American embassy at Grosvenor Square early in the morning to demonstrate their displeasure at the long delay in receiving transportation to the United States. Two women entered the embassy as representatives of the larger group and talked to Colonel Mallory of the U.S. headquarters in the United Kingdom. The representatives reported to the rest of the waiting brides that there would be no news of transportation until all American servicemen were home. They also reported that the commission, set up to examine the question of war bride transportation, would not have any concrete answers for another three to four weeks. Some of the women were facing financial problems; their husbands had returned to the United States and been demobilized, which ended military allotments. Embassy officials suggested that women in these circumstances could apply to the American Red Cross for aid, but some women stated that they had already applied and been refused. A small deputation of women then went across the street to the American Red Cross headquarters and emerged later with the promise that the Red Cross would help those women in trouble.[28]

Hundreds of wives stayed in central London so they could attend a meeting later that evening at Caxton Hall, Westminster. One newspaper estimated the crowd at several thousand. All the brides could not get into the meeting when it began but one hundred to two hundred did manage to find space within the room to listen to the United States embassy representative, Lieutenant Commander Herbert Agar. He could not answer their questions or let them know when transportation would be available but told them that the United States commission was meeting to sort out the problems. The wives vehemently declared that they were not seeking to displace returning American soldiers on transports but rather that they were protesting "'the official run-around' they had been getting in their quest for information about future transportation." However, some women did want immediate passage to the United States, especially those who were pregnant. For these women, any delay in transportation that added months to their departure date would keep their children from being born in America. Many women explained their concerns about financial problems and the housing shortage in Great Britain.[29] War brides pointed out that they should at least take priority over the transportation of entertainers and, as in one reported incident, a ship full of animals. Still other women told Lieutenant Commander Agar that since they had been working throughout the war in various capacities they could, conceivably, build their own planes or ships more quickly than the United States government could arrange transportation.[30]

The perceptions of the participants and the publicity they received complicated the situation. One war bride stated her conviction that "the British authorities are not to blame for this. They would help us if they could. The truth is that the American Government does not want us over there and is doing its best to break up our marriages." Considering the history of the army's attitude toward overseas marriage and war bride transportation, her argument was believable to many. Another bride expressed her opinion that the press had misrepresented war bride problems. She asserted that war bride "grievances are both genuine and reasonable. Perhaps the worst of them is that we feel nobody is bothering about us." This bride also said that many war brides were undergoing undue hardships as wives of American servicemen. Some friends and relatives viewed the brides as women of questionable virtue, putting them "on the same level, in fact, as the type of women who had been running around promiscuously with Allied soldiers." Long separation from their husbands was another strain on the war brides, as were the problems of allotments, housing, and medical needs. The women were eager to get on with their married lives. They were frustrated further by the apparent apathy and poor organization of government officials. Some war brides worried that lengthy separation from their husbands would result in failed marriages. They wanted a shipping priority for war brides and "a definite date, something to look forward to."[31]

The best the American government could offer the brides was a vague suggestion that transportation might well be available sometime in January 1946. In addition, officials like Lieutenant Commander Agar repeatedly told the protesting women that they were being selfish by demanding immediate transportation. The *Daily Express* had published a letter from five GIs on the day of the war bride protest in October. These servicemen expressed their desire to return to the United States and stressed that they, as fathers and husbands, had endured separation from their families for far longer than the war brides had been apart from their husbands. The GIs asked, "Now, girls, do you think you can bring yourselves to do without your husbands for a few months?" Lieutenant Commander Agar praised the wisdom of the servicemen's argument.[32] Two days later the same newspaper published a brief article from New York about reactions to the war bride protests. The story predicted that there would be considerable outrage in the United States if the government transported war brides before returning troops. The author noted, "Naturally, there is no particular love for the brides among the womenfolk here. There is a tendency to regard them as having stolen a good American boy at a time when his resistance was low. But there would be downright hatred for them if those same womenfolk felt that their boys were being held up."[33] The author erroneously reported that there had been no similar protest by the GI husbands in the United States over delays in war bride shipments, implying that the waiting husbands saw no need to speed up the process.

The war bride protests in London carried on for two or three days and fed British tabloids. With a headline announcing that "Send-us-home Wives Get Transport Shock," the *Daily Express* fell in with the mood of condemnation surrounding the war bride protests. The staff reporter noted that the information he received about transportation priorities from the American embassy was available to the wives when they spoke with Lieutenant Commander Agar earlier in the week, "if they had been in the mood to listen."[34] The reporter failed to realize that information he received from the embassy was no news to the British war brides. The question for these women was not how or who, but when. While certain government officials and news reporters could express their views on war bride transportation from what they perceived as the moral high ground, the war brides had to hang on as best they could and put their lives on hold while their futures were in the hands of strangers.

The newspapers also reported that British authorities, such as Minister of Health Aneurin Bevan, were working to expedite the emigration of the women to free up housing in Britain. Unfortunately, the newspapers exaggerated when they contended that the British government was actively pursuing a policy of aiding the war brides. Certainly the British authorities did get drawn into the question of war bride transportation, but they proceeded very reluctantly. When Mary Williams, a U.S. representative on the British American Liaison Board, recommended a publicity campaign, the British Foreign Officer agreed it was an excellent idea and noted that "we would certainly not stand in the way of the Americans making such an announcement. In fact it seems to me to be a good idea: but the Americans must do it themselves."[35]

The British government viewed the war bride situation as an American problem and was not having any more luck than the war brides in getting a clear response from the American authorities about when transportation would be available. British constituents wrote to their elected officials voicing their concern about delays in transportation for the women. When British officials, including the head of the North American Department of the Foreign Office, P. M. Broadmead, wrote to the United States embassy or other authorities, they received the standard reply that shipping was scarce and priorities put war brides low on the list.[36] The British government used United States policy statements as a basis for its correspondence with people inquiring about transportation, even those who asked whether the British government might be able to transport the brides. Correspondents often were told that "this is a United States responsibility" when they asked for help.[37]

When the war bride protests swept London in October 1945 the issue of transportation reached Parliament. Member of Parliament Driberg proposed a parliamentary question on October 15 concerning the anticipated date that war brides might expect to sail to reunion with their husbands. The Foreign Secretary replied that the United States authorities were dealing with the issue of transportation. The second half of the question, however, concerned cases where separation of husband and wife was causing "some hardship" and what the American government was doing to relieve these cases. The British authorities had already addressed this problem to American representatives but had not received an answer. Other members of Parliament were far less concerned and quickly pointed out the relative unimportance of war brides in comparison to more pressing postwar issues in Great Britain.[38]

Eventually the United States government began to consider the question of GI war bride transportation in a more structured manner. As the passage of the War Brides Act grew near and the transportation of returning American servicemen sped up, the war bride transportation commission began sorting out the details of ships' availability and shipping space. The war brides began to hear reports of definite plans for their departure from Britain. In November and December 1945 they could read British newspapers and learn of the proposed use of the *Queen Mary* and other vessels. The new year would witness the beginning of the transportation of wives on exclusive bride ships.

The British war brides' immigration was finally beginning. There were several unprecedented aspects to this immigrant saga. First, the war brides generated some of the earliest nonrestrictive immigrant legislation in twentieth-century United States history. Previously, the American government had targeted specific groups to bar them from admission. In this case, the government passed two acts aimed at admitting a select group of immigrants. Second, the United States government not only passed legislation to allow war brides entry, it also paid for their transportation to America. This unparalleled development places the war brides in a singular position in United States immigration history. Finally, the immigration of British war brides to the United States represented the largest single movement of people from Britain to America in such a short time. The movement was so large that "immigration from England for the first time in many years exceeded that of any other country."[39]

5

From the Old World to the New

We started from England in February and then ran into terrible gales on the crossing. They had tried to take the boats through stormy weather [before and] they had lost a lot of babies with diarrhea and people with seasickness. So we went south to the Azores; we didn't land but they took a southern route to avoid the bad weather. That put our landing in New York four days late and all our reservations on the trains were gone. We were tied up to the dock for four days and all the personnel vanished. . . . It was really scary, really scary.

—Rosa Ebsary

Migration scholars have often overlooked the systems that transported immigrants to the United States. This segment of the immigrant story, however, is an important one. Immigrants become immigrants from the moment they make the decision to leave home. British war brides are no exception. What makes their story unique is the unprecedented establishment, at United States government expense, of a processing and transportation system exclusively for their use. The war bride transportation system utilized by British women is one of the best-documented immigrant movements in history. In addition, each phase of the transportation network involved not only the physical movement of these female immigrants but also the beginnings of the immigrant adjustment process.

Not all war brides traveled by this method. Some British women came to America on commercial transports either by sea or air. The war brides who traveled to the United States at private expense did so for various reasons. A few managed to get to the United States before the war was over, hence, before the United States government had organized free transport. Others came to the United States privately after the war, possibly to avoid dealing with the lengthy army system or because they did not want to travel with the masses of other war brides. While women traveled to the United States in a variety of ways the overwhelming majority came on "bride ships" in the army transportation system. There were three distinct phases in the transit of British war brides who traveled in this way: their arrival and processing at a camp in Britain, their journey to America aboard bride ships, and their excursions by train to final destinations within the United States. The army had overall control of the scheme but many different agencies contributed to the arrangements.

THE EMBARKATION CAMP

The United States government had tried originally to involve the British government in the war bride transportation scheme. However, "the British declined to assume any part of the program because of an acute labor shortage."[1] Hence, the organization fell to American agencies under the direction of the Army Transport Corps. By late 1945 news began to emerge about a war bride transportation camp at Tidworth, in southern England, for the processing of women and children on their way to the United States. According to the *Daily Mail*, war brides and their children would "start their journey to the United States" by 1 January 1946. The United States Army would run the camp and provide "food, medical attention, and even entertainment" while the war brides finished their immigration processing. The American authorities claimed that they had already made arrangements for twenty-six thousand of the estimated fifty thousand British war brides who needed transportation.[2]

The camp at Tidworth was only in the planning stages in December 1945, however. The United States Army was working in conjunction with the American Red Cross to arrange the details of war bride movements. The original plan called for the army to notify war brides throughout Britain when their names came up on the travel roster. Women and children were to go by train to a central rail point at Waterloo Station in London. From there, war brides from across Great Britain would board special trains that would take them to the embarkation area. The army expected to use the Carlton Hotel at Bournemouth to house women with small children while all other dependents would stay at Tidworth barracks. The army anticipated it would take three to seven days to check war bride documents, arrange physical exams, and process the women through customs. The war brides and children would then board their designated ship for the journey to the United States. The army would be responsible for the bulk of the processing while the American Red Cross would provide guidance and counseling for women with special problems such as misplaced documents. The Red Cross would also conduct recreational and support services during the war brides' stay at Tidworth. The American Red Cross noted that Tidworth contained recreational facilities for a variety of activities including "movies, impromptu stage shows, sight-seeing tours, exhibitions, games and conversation."[3]

Although plans were progressing by December 1945, a series of meetings between personnel from the United States Army and Navy, State Department, Public Health Service, and American Red Cross revealed a number of potential problems. A Red Cross worker noted that "the plans apparently are not going forward with any great degree of smoothness and everybody is quite worried about the outcome."[4] Part of the problem was the lack of concrete information regarding ship availability. While planners had assumed a steady flow of war bride departures numbering six thousand per month, rumors of the use of large luxury liners such as the *Queen Mary* and the *Europa* created a major logistical problem since these vessels would carry many more passengers than the other designated bride ships. If the stories were true, transportation officials would need to modify their plans. The nineteen officials attending the planning meeting at the United States embassy were having no better luck than the war brides in getting concrete information about available transportation from appropriate United States government authorities. The representatives at the meeting "considered [it] to be an urgent necessity that the War Department be cabled to give some definite information as to when, how many dependents are to be shipped at a time and which ships are going to be used."[5]

As the commencement of the "War Bride Operation" in Great Britain approached, preparations for the first contingent of war brides took on formidable proportions. Colonel Thomas Houston was in charge of Tidworth Camp, and his duties including getting the barracks in shape to house women and children and overseeing final preparations for their transportation. The first group of war brides and their children were due to arrive on 22 January and would be in camp for four days. The United States Army had to provide several extraordinary services and supplies for the dependents, including building two hundred cribs and making twelve hundred diapers. The army estimated that it would eventually provide accommodations and transportation for fifty thousand brides and twenty thousand children. Part of the plan called for running the camp in such a way that the women would never have to stand in a queue, and normal army discipline was to be eased to allow for a more relaxed atmosphere. One sergeant noted that the army planned to treat "the brides . . . about the same as we treat a major." In addition, camp publicity boasted the availability of a movie theater and a large variety of food services such as separate menus for the brides, children, and pregnant women. The army also publicized restrictive measures that included taking steps to avoid incidents of stowaways. Stowaways later proved to be a small but significant problem.[6]

By January 1946, Tidworth Camp, described by one newspaper as "something like a country club for G.I. brides," was in its final stage of preparation for "Operation Atlantic" and the first ships were ready.[7] The army had outfitted the ships with necessities for babies, such as talcum powder, baby oil, special foods, cribs, diapers, facilities for heating bottles, and pink and blue blankets. The ship's company would include both army nurses and American Red Cross members to help the women while en route.[8] The only thing left was to await the arrival of the first contingent of British war brides.

When the date of departure of the first ship drew near, the United States authorities notified the war brides to begin the final phase of preparation for their journey. The army advised them that "arrangements are now being made for your passage to the United States, and you should immediately prepare yourself to travel on very short notice."[9] Women could reject or accept transportation by completing a postcard and returning it to the army. Women had to complete a questionnaire and return it to the Transport Office within forty-eight hours. The questionnaire asked for personal data such as name, address, husband's name, and whether the bride was pregnant. In addition, it provided the war brides the opportunity to list the number of baggage items they would be taking with them, the train depot nearest their home, and whether they or the American embassy held their passport. The form provided the United States Army with information necessary to arrange specific details of travel for the war brides.

An accompanying list of instructions reiterated general immigration information and the army's specific transport plans within Great Britain. As wives of American servicemen the women no longer needed a visa to travel to the United States, but visas were still necessary for all illegitimate and step-children. All women and children did need current passports, but those women who had turned their passports into the United States embassy would be able to pick them up at the staging area. The Transport Office advised the women to bring other documents for themselves and their children, including baptismal, marriage, and birth certificates. In addition, the British government required that war brides turn in their ration and clothing books and identity cards at Tidworth. Baggage weight restrictions, as determined by the United States and British authorities, allowed for two hundred pounds per adult and fifty pounds per child. The British war brides could bring used household goods duty free, and transportation of jewelry was duty free if the bride had owned the jewelry "prior to the owner's departure" and was not for resale. The war brides would have to ship any household goods above and beyond the two-hundred-pound limit at their own expense and on commercial transport. Since transportation was so scare, this last condition usually meant that war brides left Britain with only two hundred pounds of personal goods. The strict limit on baggage was necessary since the brides were traveling on recently converted troop ships with limited space. Women would have to store the remainder of their baggage in the ship's hold, including all baby carriages (prams) and trunks. Furthermore, the army disavowed any responsibility for the travelers' baggage until it reached the embarkation camp. This meant that along the route to Tidworth, war brides had to keep track of all of their personal effects.

The Transport Office informed the war brides that embarkation camp staff included medical personnel to help in case of illness and to verify vaccination certificates for all travelers.[10] In addition, instructions notified the women that they needed to carry a twenty-one-day supply of baby formula as well as food for the day they traveled to Tidworth, but that "all meals will be furnished at Army expense, from the time you arrive in Reception Area until you arrive at your final destination in the U.S." Post Exchange privileges would be available at Tidworth Camp for the war brides. The army also supplied the brides with a letter of authority to use at Bank of England locations to exchange British sterling for American dollars and would forward details of other financial transactions involving defense bonds, securities, and other instruments at the request of brides. Finally, the instructions to the war brides concerning travel to the embarkation camp included an admonition to leave all aspects of travel arrangements to the Transport Office and under no circumstances allow friends or family to accompany them on their journey to Tidworth. The army also reminded the brides that it would not provide transportation for women who were over seven months pregnant or who had children under three months of age.

Once the war brides had completed the questionnaire, returned it to the United States Army, and waded through the lengthy instructions, all they had to do was wait for notification about the day of departure. This announcement entailed another form letter and three more pages of instructions. This last notification included the specific information war brides had been waiting for. The army sent train certificates for travel to London and on to Tidworth to all British war brides outside the greater London area, complete with date and time of train departure from the station nearest their home. Army Transport Office representatives would meet the women in London and help them complete transfer to Tidworth. Most of the remaining instructions restated previous warnings, with the added advice to bring a twenty-one-day supply of any special baby needs, including items such as bottles and orange juice. The Transport Office borrowed an idea from the Canadian authorities' war bride scheme and included special baggage tags for labeling suitcases and trunks in transport to Tidworth.[11] The army again warned the war brides against arriving too early or too late. There would be no accommodation for early arrivals at the embarkation point and late arrivals risked losing their place in the transportation network. If war brides could not leave as scheduled, the army asked that they notify the Area Transport Office immediately. Under no circumstances should the women travel if their babies were ill.

The first group of British war brides to test the army transportation system arrived at Tidworth on 23 January 1946. This group included 344 women and 116 children. Members of the British Women's Voluntary Services (WVS) had assisted the brides at Waterloo Station in London. The WVS provided a reception room and refreshments while the war brides awaited the departure of the special train to Tidworth.[12] For many women this was their first opportunity to mingle with a larger group of war brides. They were finally on the way, on the first leg of the long journey that would take them to an unknowable future, to reunion with a wartime lover, and to a new country. For some women this initial stage was where they said goodbye to friends and family. Peggy Virden remembered that, despite warnings from the army, she was unprepared for the quick separation from her family. As she recalled:

> I had received notification that I was to go to Liverpool Street Station in London, so one of my brothers went with me. When we got to Liverpool Street Station there were American service personnel who took care of us and our luggage. We were to go over to Victoria Station. They loaded us on some buses and I

had to leave my brother right there and then he went on his own over to Victoria while I went on the bus with the rest of the girls. When we got to Victoria my aunt and mum were there and I had to tell them they couldn't go any further than that. My brother couldn't go any further than that.[13]

It was also a time to have the first look at other war brides. The war bride population included women from all regions of Great Britain and from many different backgrounds. This diversity surprised many war brides. Joan Posthuma remembered waiting at Waterloo Station with her mother when she spotted another war bride approaching. "Here comes this family; mother, father, brother, aunt, uncle and all and then she comes and she has this ragged fur coat on, her hair in curlers, all her clothes in a sheet, and this kid under her arm." By contrast the war bride had been talking to another war bride who "was very la-di-da. Her husband was a lieutenant colonel and she had a little boy and her people came in with a chauffeur."[14] The colonel's wife and the war bride with the sheet suitcase ended up as roommates. Although there were regional variations and a few class differences among the war brides, the majority were from working- or lower-middle-class families.

Many other surprises would follow as the war brides boarded the special trains and traveled to Tidworth barracks. The first shock for some was discovering that they would be sharing barracks with other women and children. Perhaps equally surprising was the sight of German prisoners of war who acted as stewards and groundskeepers at Tidworth. Where were the luxurious and ample accommodations? What had become of the promise of no queuing? Dinner that first night at Tidworth consisted of corned beef hash and vegetables for all, not separate menus. For food, Joan Posthuma recalled, "they used to come with this stuff. I don't know what it was, oh dear. We had this stuff on our plates and we didn't know what the heck it was."[15] Rosa Ebsary remembered that "all the work was being done by German prisoners of war and they used to come wandering in where you were sponge bathing and everything."[16] The camp situation was definitely not "as advertised." These first war brides had four days to wait before sailing; four days to complete all last-minute processing, and four days to reflect on the enormity of the step they were about to take. One wonders what the youngest war bride in this first group was thinking. What thoughts crossed the mind of the sixteen-year-old war bride while she tended her thirteen-month-old baby boy on that first night in camp?

British war bride experiences at Tidworth were far different from those portrayed in the publicity of the United States Army or the official history of the American Red Cross. The women remember a variety of events in the camp but for the overwhelming majority the ignominy of the physical exam stands out the most. Despite government regulations that eased war brides' entry into America as wives of United States citizens, they still had to undergo a physical. Rosa Ebsary spoke for thousands when she described the event as "a panic. They lined you up for a physical and, I remember, they told you to take all your clothes off and they gave you a bathrobe. I remember there was a lady, must have been in her forties, very well educated and nice lady, that was ahead of me in the line. She went in and they said, 'Open your robe' and they shone a flashlight under her arms and in between her legs. She came back and got in the line again. She didn't think that could possibly be the physical."[17]

In addition, the German prisoners who maintained the camp and mess hall frightened some of the women. June Porter recalled that an alarm went up in the middle of the night during her stay at Tidworth, signaling the escape of a prisoner. After a lengthy search the authorities discovered the "escapee" in a nearby field in the company of a British war bride from the camp.[18] There were some incidents of fraternization between war brides awaiting transportation and the men working at the camp, both German prisoners and American servicemen. Though these events were rare and most war brides blamed this type of behavior on a few "loose" women, the overall reputation of war brides suffered a further decline among the workers assigned to their care. While the extramarital activities of some war brides did not receive publicity with the populace of either Great Britain or the United States, the conditions at Tidworth Camp did generate cries of outrage from various individuals.

To the credit of the American Red Cross, some of the organization's workers brought to light several problems at Tidworth in their interagency files. In March 1946, at an informational meeting concerning Tidworth problems, American Red Cross personnel noted that some war brides had reported having to pay for their meals while in the camp. This practice meant some women ran out of money and had to ask the American Red Cross for financial assistance. The War Department representative denied the allegations although he did promise to look into the matter in more depth. The American Red Cross also voiced concern over "the barracks type of living that they have [and] the length of stay." Throughout the British war bride operation women stayed in the camp for as little as three days or as long as ten, with one group of war brides stranded at Tidworth for seven weeks. The American Red Cross noted that the longer the women stayed in camp before departure the harder the work for the Red Cross personnel who had to help women with limited resources. At the time of the March 1946 meeting the longest length of stay for a group of war brides at Tidworth had been fourteen days, which the American Red Cross believed was excessive. Delays stemmed from late ship arrivals and striking workers. Although the Red Cross representatives aired their concerns they also "agreed that there was nothing much that we could do regarding the length of stay at Tidworth."[19] Another problem involved war brides who were ill on arrival in New York and when they boarded trains for their final destination. The American Red Cross speculated that the food on board ship could be too rich and medical exams too lax, but again the War Department representative stated that there would be no changes in these areas.

This was apparently the standard response by United States government authorities to most problems encountered by war brides in the transportation process. When the American Red Cross complained of inadequate ship lists and resultant problems for war brides' families in the United States, the War Department representative "firmly said there was nothing that could be done about these lists." The meeting did result in an agreement to publicize the potential problems of ship lists and to recommend vehemently that relatives should not show up in New York to meet the ships. This latter issue had placed a burden on American Red Cross finances when ex-GIs applied for aid in New York due to delayed ship arrivals. The meeting confirmed, however, that the United States government and Red Cross "would have to endeavor to render good service in spite of many difficulties."[20]

The conditions at Tidworth attracted some outside attention as well. In April 1946 a British war bride wrote to her mother while still in camp at Tidworth. She said that "so far I have been disgusted with the arrangements" made by the United States Army and government. She raised some questions about the camp being an unfit "place for babies. I'm using least of possible of my nappies [diapers] because we have no place to boil them or dry them. . . . All we have for our use is the bed, haven't even a nail to hang my coat, however, the baby is okay. . . . There is [sic] over 900 of us nearly all with babies."[21] This war bride's mother wrote to her Member of Parliament asking that the Minister of Health investigate the conditions at the camp. She noted that she did not want any special treatment for her daughter and grandchild but that she worried about the welfare of the women and children at the camp, especially "when you read of these young babies dying from pneumonia crossing the Atlantic. I am thinking that it starts at the beginning of their journey at the Reception Center."[22]

The bride's mother was referring to newspaper stories about illness suffered by children during the war bride transportation operation. One incident, reported in the *Los Angeles Herald,* noted that "a concentration-type camp in England where brides of former American GIs await transportation to their adopted country today was blamed for the deaths of nine babies from a mysterious malady which struck them down as they arrived in New York recently." The article referred to deaths that took place on the SS *Holbrook,* which sailed from Southampton in April 1946. The War Department was reportedly investigating allegations that the babies contracted the illness while at Tidworth. The husband of a war bride went so far as to suggest that "the wives of American servicemen are treated like displaced persons. They are made to line up at 6 A.M. like soldiers, although many of them are too weak for such military routine. Their food is handled by prisoners of war and their medical examinations are routine and made by disinterested doctors."[23] The ex-soldier stated his belief that the conditions at Tidworth, not those on board the ships, caused sickness and death. The mother of a sick baby mentioned in the *Los Angeles Herald* article wrote to the British consul seeking an investigation into camp conditions at Tidworth. As with the earlier complaints, this GI bride noted the lack of facilities at Tidworth for coping with a baby's needs such as the washing and drying of diapers. She explained that her child

> began to get ill with diahera [*sic*] a few days after we arrived at the Camp and although we all had to pass a medical examination whilst at the Camp the Doctor only glanced at Alan. I was informed when I mentioned the complaint that babies before our crowd had had the same thing but they didn't seem to attach much importance to it. Whether any importance could be attached to the fact that the young lady in the Formula Room mixed double strength food for 2 feeds instead of two separate feeds being made I do not know, but it was terribly sick. During the journey on board the "Queen Mary" he began to get terribly thin and ill looking and he got steadily worse on the train journey to Los Angeles which resulted in the Doctor sending him straight to the Children's Hospital within 24 hours of arrival where he has been since.[24]

The British consulate contacted the British embassy in Washington, D.C., noting that other newspapers had printed similar stories, creating a great deal of negative publicity. The British embassy then informed the North America Department of the British Foreign Office in London, which subsequently wrote to the American embassy. The American embassy response was to pass the original British war bride letter about her sick child on to the Army Transport authorities. The American vice consul noted that the United States Army had already investigated conditions at Tidworth due to the letter sent by the young bride's mother complaining about the lack of baby facilities. The United States Army Transportation Corps report on Tidworth concluded that "the complaints of the young lady in question have been thoroughly investigated and have proved to be groundless."[25] The army's conclusion was not surprising considering its reluctance to become fully involved in the war bride phenomenon since it all began.

The deaths of nine children on the SS *Holbrook* in April 1946 were followed by a more highly publicized incident the following month on the *Zebulon Vance*, which was filled with European war brides sailing out of Le Havre. In this case seven children died, three en route and four upon arrival in New York. The additional publicity forced the United States Army to change its transportation process. From 11 June 1946 onward, all war brides over six months pregnant and all children under six months of age could not travel on United States transport. In addition, no shipment of war brides and dependents was to have more than 25 percent children under the age of six. The War Department also instructed personnel at embarkation centers to conduct more thorough medical exams on individuals awaiting transportation. Pregnant women and women with very young children, who were already in the processing phase, were hit hard by this change in procedure that disqualified them for travel.

Interestingly, the United States Army and the War Department initiated this shift in policy despite absolving themselves of all blame for the deaths on the *Zebulon Vance*. United States authorities had determined that "any deaths among the passengers . . . due to epidemics was [*sic*] not caused by any conditions or situations existent in the Port of Embarkation; nor on board ship."[26] The army concluded that the mothers were responsible for the incidents and accused them of "gross negligence."[27] Nevertheless, the army did change its policies regarding the transportation of pregnant women and young babies.

THE VOYAGE

Once a ship sailed, the war brides continued their journey under the care of the Red Cross and the United States Army. The State and War Departments had asked the Red Cross to provide assistance to the war brides in this phase of transportation. United States authorities believed it was far more practical to rely on one service club rather than calling on others such as Traveler's Aid. In late 1945 the American Red Cross began to make plans for hiring special staff to accompany war brides on the ships. With Red Cross personnel permanently assigned to specific ships, these staff members crisscrossed the Atlantic numerous times during the transportation operation. (Red Cross staff also served on ships in the Pacific that transported war brides from Australia, New Zealand, and the Philippines.) The American Red Cross estimated that each ship would need from two to three workers, depending on the ship's passenger capacity, and it intended that selection of staff for this duty would "be based solely on their work experience and their educational background insofar as these factors have pertained to recreation. . . . The workers preferably should be experienced in community recreation of a type which dealt with women and children. Graduate work in recreation would be highly desirable."[28] The army had also arranged to have a Women's Army Corps (WAC) officer and enlisted personnel on the ships for medical purposes, and the Red Cross staff would work closely with them.[29]

As late as 12 January 1946, two weeks before the first British bride ship left Southampton, the American Red Cross was still working with the army to define its representatives' on-board function. The Red Cross finally determined its major service to dependents would be to provide recreation and social services, including establishing and coordinating the operation of nurseries and playrooms. Red Cross personnel would oversee these facilities but would rely on volunteers from the passengers on board to run the programs. The social services would be equivalent to those provided at Tidworth for any war brides with specific problems. For instance, the American Red Cross anticipated that some women would be short of money since many of them were already having financial problems at Tidworth. The organization's national headquarters decided that "any financial assistance given by the Red Cross on the ship will be confined to grants of funds for necessary expenditures aboard ship."[30] If any war bride needed further financial assistance once the ship docked in New York, the on-board staff would refer them to the New York chapter of the American Red Cross Home Service division. Hence, any British war bride who had financial problems at the beginning of her journey would have to apply to three different Red Cross workers, at Tidworth, on board ship, and once docked at New York. Since the army designated New York as the primary entry point for war brides from the European Theater of Operation, the New York chapter of the American Red Cross felt the bulk of the financial strain associated with the war bride operation.

The Red Cross had planned to organize the adult recreation on board as part of its services but, in the case of the first British bride ship, the SS *Argentina,* the Army Transport Service Officer took control of this endeavor. The American Red Cross did run the recreational program for children, including a supervised playroom for youngsters old enough to participate. The playroom was open daily from nine to five but mothers who dropped off their children had to return periodically to change diapers and/or feed the children. The shipboard playroom was so successful that one supervisor recommended more Red Cross staff in this category for future voyages. The nursery also provided a much needed outlet for seasick mothers who found it difficult to care for their children. The Red Cross estimated 80 percent of the SS *Argentina* passengers fell into this category.[31] The American Red Cross also distributed warm clothing (sweaters and slacks) to numerous brides who were unprepared for the Atlantic winter, and additional baby clothes for those who did not bring enough. The organization also supplied the women with yarn and knitting needles for recreational purposes. Adult recreation on board the SS *Argentina,* often organized by army personnel, included playing games like bingo, participating in sing-alongs, viewing movies, and appearing in an amateur talent show.

The social services performed by American Red Cross personnel were perhaps the most humane aspect of their function on these ships. They handled the personal problems and emergencies of the war brides, which proved to be a heavy burden for the Red Cross person in charge. As the first ship neared New York the number of requests for aid (emotional as well as financial and legal) increased.[32] One bride had an extremely ill baby who would require hospitalization upon entry to the United States. The Red Cross in New York managed to get the husband on board when the ship docked to assist his wife with transportation of the baby to the hospital. Another bride was despondent over the previous loss of her own baby and her husband's continued struggle with "combat fatigue." The war bride explained to the Red Cross worker that in her husband's "last letters he had alternately asked for divorce, and had said he would kill himself if she didn't come to America." The worker cabled New York to try to locate the husband and determine his frame of mind. One war bride reportedly "became mentally ill" while another stayed in her bunk for the entire nine-day voyage due to a lack of proper clothing for the trip. The bride "had sold her winter clothes to get enough money to pay the 'head tax' to leave England."[33] Red Cross workers pooled their own clothing to help outfit the young bride in question. The Red Cross referred thirty-four financial cases to the New York chapter to aid war brides in completing their travel to their husbands' homes.

The bride ships sailed throughout 1946 and on-board experiences resembled those of the first brides on the SS *Argentina*. The Army Transport Authority used a variety of vessels for war bride transportation including the reconverted luxury liner *Queen Mary*. The Red Cross continued to play a major role on board the ships by supplying goods and running nurseries, while WAC personnel were in charge of orientation lectures, entertainment, and medical facilities. The GI brides on some ships put together daily newspapers (for example, "Wives Aweigh" on the *Queen Mary* and "Wives' Whispers" on the SS *Argentina*) to keep the women informed about shipboard functions and facilities and their progress at sea. These newspapers also often reported informational tidbits such as the ultimate destination of the women and children, poems written by passengers, and lists of daily activities.

Women remembering the voyages years later usually comment on two features: the crowded conditions and the abundance of food. Although the Army Transport Service had emphasized the spacious quarters on these reconverted troop ships, women usually shared rooms with eight or more other brides. Often women with children and those without were in the same room. Peggy Virden recalled her experience rooming with a woman with a small child. When it came time to retire for the evening the young mother climbed into the upper bunk adjoining Peggy's and put the baby on the outside. Peggy finally managed to persuade her to put the baby between them so it would not fall out of the bunk, but this resulted in a "dousing" each night in bed.[34] Rosa Ebsary remembered the presence of children with resentment. She stated that the Red Cross "put all of the children into nurseries and the mothers could go and see them some time during the day. . . . They asked all of the brides, in fact they almost detailed you, to wash diapers down in the hold. If you weren't seasick you got stuck with that. Well, they weren't our children. . . . I don't think that half of [the mothers] even went to visit them in the nurseries."[35] While resentment could develop in these situations, most war brides got on well together.

War brides are almost unanimous in their praise for the food on board. British women had been contending with rationing since 1939 and many of the items on board ship, especially fruit, eggs, and desserts, had been absent from their diets. Unfortunately, the richness of the food was a major contributor to seasickness among the women. In cases where ships encountered rough seas, as with the SS *Argentina,* the women remembered the difficulty of the passage itself. One woman's diary of her trip recorded that "water keeps flooding in under the doors from the decks, making the passage ways wet and slippery. A number of women have fallen."[36] Eileen Cowan remembered her battle with seasickness:

> I used to go down to the dining hall with Robbie and sit him in the high chair. They had waiters and everything. It was really nice, they were really good to us. I used to think, "Oh boy, I'm going to eat," and they would put the food in front of me and I would have to say to the guy, "Would you take care of him, I've to go out again." One day I was walking down the steps with Robbie in my arms and I fainted. I could feel myself going, it was the smell of the food. So I said to the girl next to me, "Hold him" . . . and I fell down some stairs and they took me to the doctor. The doctor examined me and he said, "Are you pregnant?" and I said "Lord, I sure hope not" because I hadn't seen my husband in nine months! I said, "No, I'm just seasick."[37]

While one war bride might recollect that the salt water made washing impossible, another remembers the first pair of slacks she ever owned, issued to her by the Red Cross.

Less "innocent" memories emerge in war bride stories about transportation as well. As with the case of fraternization between a war bride and a prisoner of war at Tidworth, the conduct of some women on the ships raised eyebrows. Disgust over the fraternization of war brides with crew members or fellow male passengers helps to explain why many war brides tried to distance themselves from the label "war bride." The stories of these cases often hurt the image of all war brides. The question remains, Were these isolated cases? The fraternization problem definitely prompted United States authorities to react. Immediately after the first ship sailed from Southampton, they issued an order banning all fraternization between ships' officers and war brides. The United States Merchant Marine War Shipping Administration order reportedly informed the men that they "must not engage in conversation with any of the brides while at sea, under penalty of immediate dismissal."[38] The issuance of the order, in conjunction with personal accounts of the war brides, clearly suggests that the problem of fraternization existed on ships. The situation was bad enough for June Porter to recall "a lot of hanky-panky going on on ours. . . . I remember crying one night, I thought 'Oh, what am I getting [into].' Suddenly it was an ugly world. . . . I can remember in my bunk, crying my eyes out, what have I done."[39] When asked about such cases, the majority of war brides do not recall any specific incidents on board. However, most women do admit that, human nature being what it is, fraternization probably did occur.

By far the most difficult problems on these voyages involved women who had left their homes in Great Britain to travel to America even though they were unsure of the reception they would receive. American Red Cross personnel noted several women on each voyage who had managed to slip through government barriers. Some men had divorced their wives before they sailed, some women had not heard from their husbands for a while, and others had received letters from their husbands advising them not to make the trip. Typical of the onboard problems handled by American Red Cross and army officials were those on the USAT *E. B. Alexander* in April and May 1946. The American Red Cross senior representative reported that there had been twenty-two social-service requests during the voyage. The organization had solved most of these problems with grants of money for expenses or by referring the women to the New York port chapter for arrangements for further travel. However, some women had more complex difficulties, as recounted in a Red Cross report:

> One passenger reported she did not have proof of her husband's divorce, so we sent a cable ahead requesting that he bring divorce papers to New York. One passenger is bringing a child, not related, to his father, since the mother deserted the child a year ago. She did not know if the father had been notified or would be in New York; thus we sent a cable on that case. She also was having trouble of her own, and does not want to go to her husband, but plans to work out a divorce plan. She is a T.B. suspect, moreover. Her case was referred to the Chapter, as well as that of the child.[40]

The number of problem cases was remarkably small in this example from the USAT *E. B. Alexander* considering it carried 510 war brides and 388 children. However, all women might not have reported their dilemmas to the American Red Cross.

The war brides' problems served to underscore the tenuous nature of many of the relationships between the British women and their GI husbands. One bride on board the SS *Argentina* noted in her diary as she approached New York that "my husband is coming up to fetch me [from Mississippi]. I haven't seen him for nearly eighteen months, and he has never seen his year-old daughter."[41] While American Red Cross personnel marveled that there had been relatively few difficulties in the first month of operation, one home service director did record her concern "for the girl whose husband has divorced her. What is her status? The Military contends that in instances where divorce is indicated, we should contact Immigration and have the girl sent from the ship to Ellis Island pending investigation."[42] The American Red Cross had to address each case individually. One war bride arrived in New York only to discover that her husband refused to accept her and their child. The Red Cross investigated the situation and discovered that the woman had known her husband was no longer interested but had decided to make the trip anyway. In addition, the Red Cross inquiries revealed that the husband had moved in with another woman since his return to the United States and was currently in jail for theft. The bride insisted on going to her husband's hometown of Bowling Green, Kentucky, and eventually moved in with her husband and mother-in-law. However, the man continued to date other women and the war bride became the sole means of support for her new "family" by working at a local department store.[43]

Yet another bride arrived in New York a month after her husband had divorced her. She had known of the divorce but was "determined to come to the United States. Since she was an orphan she was reluctant to return to England and said she has an offer of marriage from a veteran . . . whose present address is Sacramento."[44] The American Red Cross cabled the ex-serviceman in California and he replied that he was willing to marry the British woman and was on his way to New York. The American Red Cross was unsure as to the woman's status in the United States. The organization tried to help women with problems by determining the nature of disputes and the options open to them in various situations. Marital problems involved women arriving to discover they had been divorced and men denying that a marriage had ever occurred. One American Red Cross worker captured the poignancy of the war brides' situation when he noted that the "Number of Individuals Served" does not reflect the drama in the moment of the brides [*sic*] meeting her civilian American soldier husband in his country, nor the expression in the husband's eyes as the Red Cross worker hands to him for the first time—his baby. Neither does it reflect the sincerity in the simple nod of appreciation as the worker directs them to the next step in their pier clearance and returns to the ship to help another.

The statistical report will not reveal the tragedy in the eyes of the bride who debarked in a strange land alone, leaving to others the detail of caring for the remains of her baby which died during the voyage. It will not reveal the silence with which one father received his baby whose mother had died from childbirth in England, nor will it reveal the kindness and the sympathy with which a Red Cross worker calls a bride into a quiet corner and tells her that her husband refuses to accept her and that divorce proceedings have begun.[45]

It is important to remember that the majority of British war brides landing in New York did not have these types of problems. Most had happy reunions with their GI husbands.

When the first British war brides arrived in New York on the SS *Argentina* after nine days at sea, publicity about them was intense and certainly unprecedented for any other immigrant group. A variety of New York City newspapers devoted several pages to the trip with photographs of the brides, the children, and the husbands who had come to the port to meet them. The news coverage lasted two days and covered every imaginable angle of the story. The SS *Argentina* carried 626 passengers (451 brides and 175 children) and a merchant marine crew of 278. In addition, there were 4 Red Cross staff on board, 41 men and women from the army, and numerous reporters and photographers.[46]

Banner headlines ranging from "Stork Ship Brings GI Wives and Babies" to "Here Come the Brides" announced the 6:00 A.M. docking of the SS *Argentina* at New York Pier 54. The ship's arrival generated both excitement and confusion. Debarkation procedures were untried and the presence of the journalists added to the disorder. The *New York Times* reported that the wives "stood the strain well and endured with remarkable patience an invasion of 200 newspaper reporters, still photographers, radio men and newsreel cameramen who were permitted aboard . . . with free rein to roam the corridors, enter the packed cabins, and amid the packing and babycrying, garner biographical sherds about the 'new colonists' from England."[47] Reporters filed stories about the myriad events on this first official war bride voyage, such as the rough seas and the passengers' seasickness. Many newspapers picked up on this unpleasant aspect of the trip. The account of one small child who almost fell overboard during the voyage also attracted the reporters' attention.

The majority of publicity surrounding this and other voyages was extremely positive. Newspapers filled their pages with photographs of women and children preparing to meet waiting husbands and fathers. The photos depicted women putting on makeup, feeding babies, changing diapers, and lining the rails of the arriving ship. Certainly the residents of New York in February 1946 could not have failed to learn that a new contingent of immigrants had reached America's shores. These first British war brides handled it well; they prepared for debarkation but took the time to answer reporters' questions. As one newspaper proclaimed, however, there were

> LOTS MORE TO COME. Newspaper photographers have given us ample evidence that the Argentina, first of the family fleet carrying G.I.s' foreign brides, has made port safely after storms. The evidence is so prolific that a warning is in order if there is to be any film left for the thousands yet to come. . . . though there may be some diminution in public welcomes when shiploads of brides are no longer novelties, there will be none in the welcome of individual G.I.s impatiently awaiting the working of a solemn system of priorities governing the order of the wives' arrival.[48]

For some lucky brides the trip ended in the New York area, where eager husbands met them. Reunions between wives and husbands, especially for the first few ship arrivals, were often chaotic. The American Red Cross and the Army Transport Service planned to reunite some war brides and husbands at the Red Cross chapter house in New York, not on the pier. This was the plan for women who were to live in the New York area and those whose husbands could get to New York to pick them up. All other brides would travel from the ship to railway stations the day after the ship docked, then head by train to their final destinations. To avoid dockside confusion, the army and the State and War Departments, as well as the Red Cross, had publicized their intention to transport brides anywhere in the United States for free. This plan fell apart from the start, however.

Some ships arrived in New York late, others early. The transportation authorities' decision to inform husbands of the exact name of their wives' ships and the date of arrival in New York only after the ships had sailed from Southampton was a problem. Many husbands ignored the suggestion to stay home and, instead, traveled to New York City when they thought their wives' ships were likely to arrive. Passenger lists were often inaccurate. Any last-minute changes to the ship roster meant added confusion. Husbands sometimes arrived to meet wives who were not on board; war brides often waited for men who had no idea they had made it onto the ship.

The late arrival of the first bride ship, the SS *Argentina*, set a pattern of turmoil. Many husbands ignored the official order to meet passengers at the Red Cross chapter house on Lexington Avenue. They showed up at the pier instead. Newspapers carried reports of some GI husbands who tried to get on board the ship, two of whom succeeded before being discovered and escorted away. Other husbands waited out the hours at the chapter house. One ex-GI told reporters "he had been to the chapter house twice before, 'once last Friday, but the boat wasn't in' and again yesterday."[49]

Eventually the dockside turmoil subsided and, seven hours after the ship arrived, the first busload of women from the SS *Argentina* arrived at the chapter house, where over two hundred husbands waited. The Red Cross plan called for each woman to approach the dais singly and have her name read over the loudspeaker after which she would reunite with her husband. This system also broke down as soon as the first group of women got off the bus and the war brides and GIs began wandering the room looking for each other. The *New York Times* reported that "all was confusion. Blinking in the glare of the powerful lights that had been set up by the newsreel cameramen, the brides entered the auditorium. Babies cried. Husbands elbowed one another aside as they spotted the face they had been waiting to see."[50] Of the 451 war brides on the SS *Argentina*, approximately 200 met their husbands in New York.

Debarkation was not the end of the story, however, for the remaining 251 war brides. The next step was the journey by train; the passengers included women destined for forty-six of the forty-eight states. Since the ship was late, these war brides traveled by train on the same day the ship docked rather than the day after arrival, as the American Red Cross and army plan had specified. In New York on that first day, "by 5 P.M. there were left only two unclaimed brides, and six brideless husbands" at the Red Cross chapter house.[51] The Red Cross managed to clear up the situation by securing transportation for the two brides and finding the six missing women—three on board ship and three at railway stations awaiting trains to their husbands' hometowns.

THE TRAIN TRIP

War brides traveled by rail to the most distant points in the United States and to all the states in between. The original plan called for special "war bride trains" consisting of cars attached to regularly scheduled trains. Following normal routes, the trains out of New York would travel to rail hubs such as Chicago where war brides would transfer in smaller groups to rail cars headed toward their final destinations. While the United States government paid for this phase of the journey and the United States Army arranged for the tickets and schedules, it was up to the American Red Cross workers to accompany the war brides on the trains and to arrange for help at the stations along the way. The workers were to "provide personal escort and counseling service, supplement comfort supplies furnished by the Army such as stationery, games, maps, reading material and sanitary items, give emergency financial assistance and notify chapters at transfer points of the expected arrival of war brides."[52]

The initial rail transport operation for the SS *Argentina* passengers disclosed many flaws in the system. The American Red Cross workers on board the trains out of New York noted that the time it took for the brides to debark from the ship and then finally leave by train was excessive. While debarkation began at approximately 1:30 P.M., several of the trains did not leave Penn Station until 8:30 that evening. By the time the women had reunited with their baggage and settled into their berths on board the trains it had been almost twelve hours since they had last eaten. Officials on the trains had to make special arrangements for warming baby bottles and mixing formulas as well as for the care of women and children who were ill. The Red Cross workers in charge of handling these myriad problems often had little or no rest.

Additional problems arose as the war bride trains began to arrive at transfer points. When the first bride train pulled into Chicago with twenty-four war brides and eighteen children, no army or American Red Cross representatives met the train to help with transfers and baggage. The task was beyond the resources of the lone Traveler's Aid representative at the station. To make matters worse, another contingent of newsmen and photographers descended on the war brides to garner human-interest stories for their publications. These first British war brides must have felt overwhelmed at this point; their

emotional ordeal had been going on for two weeks under the watch-
ful eyes of hundreds of strangers. It was no wonder that "at this stage
the women[,] tired, dirty[,] and hungry[,] began to cry, their one and
only big fear was that they would be left without someone to look after
them."[53] Eventually local Red Cross volunteers arrived and the war
brides completed their transfers to other trains and other stations to
begin the last leg of their trip.

The American Red Cross reports of the early train journeys are a
catalog of snafus and miscalculations. On one train a child lapsed into
a coma and the Red Cross had to locate a doctor at the next stop
willing to come on board and conduct an examination. Some brides
had incorrect tickets that needed amending so they could continue
on the right train and at the correct time. When one contingent of
brides arrived in Chicago, the Red Cross failed to provide transportation to another station, so small groups of the women loaded into
several taxis for a hair-raising ride across town. On one occasion a war
bride lay sleeping while the train arrived at her station and then
departed with her still on board, requiring hurried phone calls and
alternate plans. This was particularly noteworthy since it took place
in Maine during February and the waiting husband had to make a
three-mile trip by sleigh to pick up his bride and baby.[54]

The help and care given to war brides by Red Cross representatives took many forms, including shopping trips to Marshall Field's
during a long layover in Chicago, a bus tour of Chicago, and a night
out in New York to see Carmen Miranda. Unfortunately, the Red
Cross could not anticipate every problem. Joan Posthuma, on her way
to Dallas, had a memorable stopover at the St. Louis train depot. The
group of war brides on her train had a lengthy delay at the station
and, she recalled,

> some people in St. Louis brought buses in and took all the girls
> who didn't have babies or children, out for the day . . . but we
> got left on the station. . . . We prowled around the station for
> hours. . . . I remember there were drinking fountains. One said
> "colored" and the other "white." We were trying to get colored
> water out of this. Nobody had told us about this, nobody had
> warned us. Then there were the toilets, white and colored, so
> we went in to the colored; we wanted to see a colored com-
> mode. We really thought, "This is America, the land of every-
> thing." . . . This very nice lady came up and she told us very
> nicely that she thought we didn't realize that the toilets were
> for colored people, and the drinking fountains. So here we are

looking at her with bright stares, you see, what did she mean, "colored people"?[55]

The first glimpses of aspects of American society shocked many war brides. However, the hectic pace of travel to their new homes did not allow time for deep reflection in those first days.

Most war brides remember more pleasant aspects of their train journeys. They could use the maps distributed by the Red Cross to chart their progress across the United States. Railroad employees and other passengers aboard most trains were eager to talk to them and point out features of the countryside. The biggest problems, however, were financial. Some brides quickly ran out of money due to numerous unexpected expenses such as tipping porters, food servers, and taxi drivers, as well as the cost of meals en route. These unforeseen expenses prompted the American Red Cross to compile a chart to be used in advising war brides before leaving Britain about the projected costs associated with the train leg of their journey. The chart listed the number of days it would take to reach each state from New York and the amount of money an adult and a child would need to purchase meals. For example, North Carolina was reachable in one day by train, requiring an estimated five dollars for an adult and three dollars for a child. A four-day train ride to Washington State, however, would cost twenty dollars for an adult and twelve dollars for a child. These added expenses accrued despite the army's earlier assurance to the brides that the United States government would meet all necessary expenses on their trip.[56]

One last unforeseen problem occurred when British war brides reached their final destinations. These women were at the point of reuniting with men they had met and married under completely different circumstances. Brides had not seen their husbands for months, perhaps even a year or more in some cases. The majority of the women had never seen their husbands out of uniform. The first glimpse from the train or the first sighting on the station platform frequently brought home the enormity of the step these women had taken. Margaret Rippe remembered that "one girl got off in Idaho and her husband had the biggest hat on, one of those cowboy hats. I slept that night dreaming [mine] had one." Her husband did not show up with a cowboy hat but he did arrive at a station stop earlier than expected. She admitted that "you wanted to look your best and he hadn't told me . . . so there I was, no makeup, the messiest piece of goods."[57]

For Joan Posthuma, her unease over her decision to move to America increased on her long train ride to meet her husband. She remembered the vastness of the countryside but also the isolation. "We got into Texas first and the train stopped in the middle of nowhere and here comes this guy with these boots on and this great big hat. You see this girl, . . . they told her she *had* to get off. That was her husband. She said 'No way. I am going home. There isn't anything, there's no house.' Anyway, we persuaded her and she got off . . . but it was horrifying. . . . This was happening all the time. This happened all the way along. . . . We were all wondering what in the world we had gotten ourselves into."[58] Whatever the wives had anticipated about husbands or life in America, the reality was often unforeseen; the reunion could be smooth or shocking. The first step in assimilation for the British war brides, after immigrating across thousands of miles, was a personal confrontation with expectations.

Many of the difficulties on the first ship and train journeys improved as the system for war bride transportation continued throughout 1946. Some issues were resolved after the Red Cross managed to convince the United States Army that war bride transportation required special consideration. In October 1945 the army informed the American Red Cross that it "desire[d] *no regular* social services rendered to dependents which might at any point slow up movement. Plan is to be considered as a mechanical troop movement to be handled by Army with greatest speed and facility and *not* a Red Cross Social Service program. . . . The Army believes that such a bulk movement is an Army function and is considered primarily as similar to a movement of able-bodied troops."[59] Within five months, however, the army had begun to change its policy, and the American Red Cross noted that "the military is improving its service, and has changed its point of view to some extent: viz. W[ar] B[ride]s cannot be treated as GIs nor as crates of oranges, but have to be looked after as dependents of servicemen."[60] With this improved attitude and the valuable lessons learned from the earliest trips, the war bride transportation operation functioned more smoothly. There were still occasional problems, especially when the transportation operation expanded to include brides from the continent and the Mediterranean Theater of Operations. Military and Red Cross authorities then faced language problems associated with war brides from non-English-speaking countries.

Eventually the flood of British war brides who traveled through the transportation system reduced to a trickle. As early as mid-1946 the army and the Red Cross began considering the end of the war bride operation in the United Kingdom. Red Cross headquarters generally agreed that it would remain an active participant only as long as the War Department continued to supply specific ships designated to transport mainly war brides. After this point, local overseas chapters of the International Red Cross could perform the remaining duties. Tidworth Camp closed on 15 October 1946, shortly after the last official war bride ship, the *Henry Gibbons,* left Southampton. At this point there was "a small staff of Army men . . . in the U.K. for the purpose of issuing travel warrants and arranging shipping for war brides."[61] The army expected to continue operating this way for approximately six months, after which time any remaining British war brides would have to arrange their own transportation and then apply to the United States government for reimbursement. The army relieved the American Red Cross of all its shipboard duties on 12 November 1946.[62] The War Department press release about the discontinuance of official war bride ships in Great Britain stressed that women could still get assistance from the army to help them find commercial transportation.

Approximately seventy thousand British war brides immigrated to the United States, many of whom traveled through this transportation system. Their physical movement was unprecedented in American immigration history. The United States government paid for their transportation from the door of their homes in a town or village in Britain to the door of their husbands' homes in America. In addition, the government provided them with the means of transportation in the form of "bride ships" and "bride trains." Equally unusual was their reception in America. The vast amounts of publicity generated by their arrival in the United States was unprecedented. If any group of immigrants should have felt welcomed by America, this was it.

There is another category of women, however, who do not fit into the British war bride immigrant story. This group includes those war brides who never made it to the United States or who, immediately upon arrival, returned to the United Kingdom. The account of these "incomplete immigrants" is a significant part of the war bride story. There are no statistics in any of the official agencies relating to this segment of the war bride population, but there were a number of groups and individuals who had to handle the problems associated with British war brides whose wartime romances did not end in immigration to American and happy reunion with their GI husbands.

6

Transatlantic Divorce, Paternity, and Incomplete Immigration

[In my cabin] was a Cockney girl, and I thought she was
so rough. I didn't understand her. She was older and
obviously married a GI for the wrong reasons, but the
point was she was rough. I could remember she was tell-
ing dirty jokes. I was quite impressed with her because
I had never seen anything or heard anything like it before. She was left, he never came. . . . I remember because she was crying. I asked what's going to happen and
they said, "Well, they will take her back."

—June Porter

Even before the transportation of British war brides got underway, it
became clear that some relationships and marriages had failed to
prosper. Some alliances between GIs and British women had not resulted in marriage but had produced children. Government agencies
in the United States and the United Kingdom had to address the
concerns of GIs and British women who found themselves in unhappy
situations. Problems such as divorce and bigamous marriages, as well
as questions of illegitimacy, maintenance, and desertion, burdened
the workloads of authorities on both sides of the Atlantic. The American government followed its course of distancing itself from any
responsibility for soldiers' actions, while the British government
fought a new war with an old ally to protect the rights of a segment
of its citizenry. Neither government achieved all of its objectives in
these cases, but the United States government especially stands out
in its callous disregard toward the problems of British women.

OVERSEAS DIVORCE

Marriages that began to fall apart did so for various reasons, including incompatibility and fear of emigration. Other war bride groups experienced similar problems, which surfaced during the war. For instance, a number of Australian war brides complained as early as December 1943 that their GI husbands had deserted them. The cases in Australia were particularly difficult since Australian women who married foreigners were under legal restrictions in filing for divorce or suing for maintenance. These restrictions meant that Australian war brides could obtain a divorce only by going to or hiring a lawyer in the United States.[1] Similar problems occurred in every theater of operation. War brides who had not heard from their husbands often petitioned government authorities for help in securing financial and legal aid. Some GIs, on the other hand, sought help to extricate themselves from their commitments. Wartime marriages often occurred between couples who were virtual strangers. For example, one case in the Chaplain Corps files involved a request for aid in securing an annulment for a GI who admitted that he had shipped out twenty-five minutes after the wedding ceremony and had never lived with his British bride. In this instance the war bride was seeking to block the annulment proceedings. Although the marriage had taken place sixteen months before, the wife had never received any allotment or insurance benefits.[2]

Both GIs and war brides initiated divorce proceedings. The courses of action open to British war brides wishing to divorce American GIs while the war was in progress were relatively clearcut. The United States recognized the jurisdiction of British civil courts over an American soldier except when civil action could detain him physically or when he could not be present in court to defend himself due to his military duties and obligations. If British courts found an American GI was indebted to a British subject, then the United States Army would allow the court to notify his commanding officer, who would in turn inform the GI that he had to comply with the court ruling or risk disciplinary action. In cases where British courts had awarded judgments for alimony or maintenance, the GI's commanding officer would suggest the soldier apply for an allotment deduction from his pay (for enlisted ranks only). If a soldier did not voluntarily apply for the allotment then his wife, child, or the legal representative of either could apply directly to the army.[3]

British subjects wishing to take legal action against GIs faced many problems. One case, involving a British man attempting to serve civil papers on an American GI as corespondent in a divorce suit, helps illustrate this point. This individual, unable to locate the American GI, wrote to a Member of Parliament, who subsequently contacted the Foreign Office. The British subject and his lawyer had "been seeking to serve a legal document on an American soldier" for seven months, yet they were "consistently prevented from seeing him at each successive address" and had not received any help from United States Army headquarters. The Briton's solicitor finally received a reply from the United States Army in September 1944 informing him that the soldier "was no longer located in the United Kingdom . . . [and] presumably no British court would assert personal jurisdiction over American soldiers who are not served with process in the United Kingdom."[4] Clearly the solicitor would have served process in Britain had the United States Army been more cooperative. This uncooperative attitude of American authorities forestalled some British subjects from taking legitimate legal action.

Once an American GI had returned to the United States, pursuit of civil action in Britain was useless. The only avenue open to British women was to have the case tried in United States courts, a costly and impractical course of action. The War Department made it clear that any civil proceedings brought against American soldiers in Britain, "in which the interests of the United States are not involved," was the responsibility of the complainant.[5] The British government protested but there was nothing it could do to force the United States government to assist in the prosecution of civil actions against United States citizens. Hence, British women looked to the British government for help in achieving legal redress.

While divorce and annulment cases arose during the war, the vast majority took place in the postwar months, after the GI returned to the United States and before the wife immigrated to America. The reasons GIs initiated divorce proceedings were often complex and certainly varied. Memories of Great Britain faded for many men when they returned to the United States and the familiar surroundings of home. Some men came back to America only to discover overwhelming opposition from family members to the prospect of a foreign-born daughter-in-law. Other men returned to lives that had included American girlfriends whose no-longer-distant faces rekindled old love affairs. An army counselor, quoted in the pages of *Yank* magazine, related the tale of one recently discharged GI who had "a fiancee in Iceland and a wife and baby in England but wants to throw the three of them over for a gal in West Virginia."[6] The overseas wartime marriages that began to dissolve in the months immediately after the war caused considerable difficulty for the authorities.

Two interrelated problems confronted the women and, hence, the British government: desertion and divorce. British authorities' most pressing concern was to develop a uniform procedure to help these women. Both the Foreign and Home Offices became involved in addressing these problems. First, the British government had to determine the legal rights of British women being divorced by husbands residing in a foreign country. Second, the British authorities needed to develop a scheme to help abandoned women in financial difficulties so they could meet the costs of court actions. The problem of legal rights of the foreign resident in a divorce action was complex in the case of British war brides and GIs. Each American state (and often individual counties within a state) had separate divorce laws. The Foreign Office collected information on divorce proceedings for all forty-eight states and Alaska and Hawaii from its consular offices. It was developing a uniform policy for dealing with divorce proceedings in the United States by March 1946.

The variety of state procedures complicated the establishment of a clear policy. Not all states required the husband to notify his wife at the beginning of divorce petitions, especially if she lived outside the immediate region. Often husbands could simply put a notice in a local newspaper to begin the divorce process. In the case of overseas brides, notification through normal mail service gave "inadequate time for the defendant in the United Kingdom to retain a local lawyer in the United States and to enter an appearance and file a defence within the time limits prescribed."[7] The Foreign Office attempted to make arrangements with local American courts whereby they would notify the nearest British consul if an American filed a divorce suit against a British subject resident in the United Kingdom. This strictly voluntary system was not always successful. The only other alternative would have been a treaty between Great Britain and the United States that would have to pass Congress. British government authorities believed that negotiating a treaty would be impossible considering the reluctance of the United States government to get involved in these cases in the first place.

An additional factor, which involved meeting the cost of legal actions against British war brides, was equally difficult for the British government to address. A British war bride needed to present her side of the divorce case if she wished to contest the divorce or ask for maintenance. While most states put the burden of court costs on the husband because he was usually the sole support, this did not include the cost of a deposition. Hence, child support and alimony cases proved to be difficult to pursue. The major hurdle was, again, the diversity of state laws and the necessity of enforcing any judgments on an international scale. On one hand, British women had a better chance of receiving awards of support if the divorce took place in a United States court. Awards made by British courts were subject to protracted adjudication in America as a method of protecting the citizenry from potentially biased foreign legal systems. However, winning an award from a United States court was one thing and collecting the money was another. No enforcement agency existed to compel the ex-GIs to pay their ex-wives.

It is unclear how many British war brides living in Britain gained judgments of support in cross-Atlantic divorce proceedings. British women were at a distinct disadvantage in these proceedings, since they were unable to represent their cases in person and the American courts tended to lean toward the side of the ex-serviceman. The United States government was again unwilling to get involved directly. M. E. Bathurst of the British embassy noted, "This Embassy has approached the State Department and asked for advice on how the difficulties of these G.I. Brides may be eased. No reply has been received from the State Department, but, from conversations I have had there on this subject, I think it is likely that their attitude will be that this problem is one of the inevitable incidents of war and that the Federal Government can do nothing to affect the administration of justice in the various States."[8]

Alternatively, British war brides could initiate divorce proceedings under the terms of the Matrimonial Causes (War Marriages) Act of 1944. This act stipulated that women could file for divorce from foreign-born husbands as long as they had never lived with their husbands in his country. This applied only to marriages that took place in the United Kingdom during the war years. However, most abandoned wives were in a difficult financial situation, having lost dependent allotments when the majority of the GI husbands left the armed forces. The British government made arrangements for these war brides to receive help with legal costs under provisions of the Poor Persons Procedure. To qualify for assistance with legal expenses a war bride had to have an income of less that £2 per week and could not own capital exceeding £50. British women would have to pay a £5 deposit for items such as witnesses' expenses. The system generally allowed war brides to obtain free legal aid.[9]

Despite these mechanisms to aid British war brides, their legal position was grim. The British consulate general of Chicago summed up the situation in an address in Washington, D.C., in March 1946, when he suggested that the

British should face the facts; and the facts are that marriage and divorce laws in the United States are in a chaotic condition with no semblance of equity or justice, or even decency. . . . I suggest that we must also recognize that there is nothing we can do about it. . . .

Wives of Americans, if they are resident abroad, had better reconcile themselves to the fact that, whatever the State law may be, they can be divorced at their husbands' pleasure without even the formality of being advised that they are being, or have been divorced and also, again whatever the state laws, that if they are awarded alimony they have little chance of ever collecting it.[10]

The consul's inquiry into the issue of GI brides, based on discussions with American divorce judges, led him to speculate that as many as 85 percent of these overseas marriages would end in divorce, a number later proven to be wrong. Archival materials of the war years convey little concern for the question of divorce, which suggests a low wartime divorce rate between British war brides and GIs. The issue of divorce did not generate the publicity that wartime marriages and transportation had. It seems reasonable to conclude that, had there been a large number of divorces taking place in the war years, the United States Army would have wanted to publicize them as another method of discouraging overseas marriages. The low number of wartime divorces is also attributable to the fact that any potential marital problems would not surface until couples had an opportunity to establish a domestic relationship or until the war had ended and the marriages began to appear hasty or ill-advised to the participants. Hence, divorce proceedings, which were taking place in the United Kingdom as late as 1948, were a postwar phenomenon. In mid-1947 the Foreign Office estimated the "total number of distressed cases of women and children (legitimate and illegitimate) . . . at about 6,000."[11] Unfortunately, it is not clear how many were children and whether "distressed" meant still awaiting transportation. The American Red Cross reported 1,133 war brides remaining in Britain in July 1947 who did not wish to immigrate.[12] Therefore, the number of British war brides abandoned or divorced while still resident in the United Kingdom is impossible to determine with any certainty.

PATERNITY

British women attempting to establish paternity and collect child support faced many of the same legal problems present in cases of divorce. The United States government was reluctant to get involved in these issues as well, which meant British women confronted a system weighted against them. The first priority for unwed mothers of GI children was to establish legal paternity. During the war, if the GI willingly acknowledged the child as his, the mother could receive a dependent allotment from the GI's military pay. If the serviceman refused to acknowledge responsibility for the child then the burden of proof of paternity fell to the woman. Questions of paternity and child support that arose after the war were perhaps due to postwar employment problems. A large number of British women lost their wartime jobs and faced a situation where child support became a financial necessity.

Some women contacted the United States War Department to determine how far it would go to aid them in pursuing cases of paternity. Most of these women were requesting addresses of ex-servicemen. The War Department was very reluctant to divulge addresses of veterans unless, in the case of enlisted men, the request was for "a good reason." The War Department would give out a soldier's military address or an ex-serviceman's last known address only if it believed a case warranted it. The War Department refused to "return a soldier to a foreign country for the purpose of consummating marriage whether or not pregnancy or paternity exists." If the soldier was an officer, on the other hand, the War Department would not give out his address under any circumstances. It would forward letters from women to the men in question but, if the officer had left the armed forces, "she is advised that there is nothing the War Department can do."[13]

The British government attempted to obtain some form of recompense for its citizenry in this situation as it did in the area of divorce. In a Parliamentary Question in October 1946, a member asked the government what steps it was taking concerning getting the United States government to help provide maintenance for children. The British government acknowledged the unlikelihood of "secur[ing] the enforcement in the United States of U.K. affiliation orders" and announced its attempts to get the United States government to establish a fund to provide for the care and maintenance of the children.[14] While the legality of wife maintenance was easily proven in court with the certificate of marriage, maintenance for illegitimate children was another matter. The burden of proof of paternity rested with the woman in a classic case of her word against his. The alleged father, furthermore, needed to be able to defend the allegations. Many American states' laws required that women filing paternity or affiliation proceedings must live in the state. Eventually the United States government rejected the idea of establishing a fund for illegitimate children of American ex-servicemen in Great Britain, in part because of the bad precedent it would establish.[15]

The British government approached the American Red Cross for assistance in these cases but the Red Cross was unwilling to get involved. It recommended that the British government seek assistance from the International Migration Service instead. That agency was "prepared to make the necessary inquiries in cases referred to them by the Family Welfare Association of Great Britain." The British government even managed to secure the United States War Department's agreement to provide the International Migration Service with the "last-known civilian address of the men."[16] The International Migration Service (later renamed the International Social Service) requested that all inquiries be directed through a British welfare society rather than the British government to obtain as much pertinent information as possible through the means of a welfare case interview. According to the International Migration Service, "the minimum information required . . . includes details of how well the girl was acquainted with the alleged father, whether he was received in her home and whether there was any assumption of prospective marriage, accompanied by available documentary proof or acknowledgement of paternity."[17]

Another possible means of securing support for illegitimate children and deserted wives emerged through British government inquiries to the United States Veteran's Administration. If an ex-serviceman was collecting veterans benefits such as "disability compensation, training pay or subsistence allowance" then his wife or illegitimate children could petition the Veteran's Administration for a portion of those benefits as long as they had legal proof of the man's obligation. For an abandoned wife this meant a copy of the marriage certificate and copies of birth certificates of any children from the marriage. In the case of illegitimacy, the claimant had to have "documentary evidence that paternity has been admitted or can be proved."[18] This left the unwed mother with the same problem she had faced all along, proving paternity. In addition, fearing inundation by requests from women overseas, the Veteran's Administration, in conjunction with British authorities, did not publicize this potential source of funds. Instead, it provided various welfare agencies within Britain with information to pass on to women who might qualify for this aid. The lawyer for the Veteran's Administration "recognized the danger of widespread publicity of these funds."[19]

Despite its attempts to locate a welfare agency willing to handle these cases, the British government eventually had to take an active role in the process of establishing paternity. By 1947 part of this procedure entailed sending a letter to an ex-serviceman in the United States to inquire about the GI's intentions toward a woman who had identified him as the father of her child. The British government was careful to formulate a standardized letter that would not be "libelous." The difficulty for the British government was that "in some cases we have very little evidence indeed to support the allegations." The British plan called for the hand delivery of a double-sealed envelope marked "personal and confidential" in which the local consul had enclosed a completed form letter that stated:

> I have been given to understand that during the period of your service in the United States Armed Forces in the United Kingdom you contracted relations with a Miss _____ of _____. It is stated that you are the father of Miss _____'s illegitimate child. . . . It would be appreciated if you could state what your intentions towards Miss _____ are. Miss _____'s financial situation is an extremely poor one and failure to provide any contribution for the maintenance of her child is causing her extreme hardship.[20]

The overriding concern of all the agencies was the effect that an allegation of paternity might have on the man and his current family in the United States. The British and American governments were far more concerned about not injuring the alleged father's sensibilities than they were about gaining compensation for the mother. In addition, authorities seemed to be making moral judgments about the women in out-of-wedlock pregnancy and not the men.

By 1948 a method for pursuing legal cases against American ex-servicemen by women in Great Britain was well established, if somewhat useless. The Home Office issued instructions to various groups and agencies that British women might contact while initiating proceedings against American ex-servicemen for wife or child support. The instructions included a description of the available legal aid in case the American husband sued for divorce. If a woman sought to locate an ex-GI, she had to contact American government officials. If the woman was seeking financial support, she had to provide as much information as possible regarding her marriage to or, in the case of illegitimacy, sexual relationship with the ex-serviceman. The British consul nearest the man's home would then approach him but the British government recognized that "there is no means of com-

pelling the man to do anything and the Consul must rely on persua-
sion."[21] The outlook for British women seeking redress from discharged American servicemen was dismal. By mid-1948 the British
government had concluded that "if the man does not respond in the
first instance to a moral appeal, there is little prospect of securing
maintenance for abandoned wives or illegitimate children. We found
that a voluntary contribution has been obtained in only about one
per cent of the total cases."[22]

Without the firm commitment of both governments, British wom-
en were largely unable to gain child support. The exact number of
American servicemen who fathered illegitimate children in Great
Britain during World War II is unknown. Even more difficult to cal-
culate is the number of British women who successfully sued for support for either themselves or their children, legitimate or otherwise.
In early 1946 the Foreign Office admitted that "British authorities had
no definite information as to the numbers of married women or
mothers of illegitimate children who might be left without support
from American GI husbands upon demobilization."[23]

A corollary to the issue of paternity and child support was the case
of the adoption of illegitimate children by their American fathers or
other relatives. Government officials had approached the American
Red Cross but it refused to become involved since its personnel felt
that their participation would require "knowing about the proposed
home for the child and whether suitable plans had been worked out
for his reception."[24] The Red Cross did contact other organizations
in an attempt to establish a procedure for the arrival of illegitimate
children in the United States. Officials of the United States Children's
Bureau met frequently with American Red Cross personnel and agency representatives but, again, the Army and War Departments refused
to participate. They insisted that they would only "provide escort
services to *legitimate* children of service personnel," creating a clear
distinction between cases of legitimate and illegitimate birth.[25] The
use of the term "escort services" implies that some children of GIs
did travel to the United States, but these could have been legitimate
children only.

If any GI established paternity and acknowledged that he was the
father of a child, American citizenship was automatically conferred
on the child. The next step in these cases was for the British mother
to relinquish her custody. This was often not a problem if the woman had a British husband. The British government regarded the adoption of illegitimate children by United States citizens as a good thing.
British authorities instructed welfare agencies to conduct background

investigations to determine the local circumstances that would greet each child. The overall philosophy of the British government was that these children, on the whole, would be better off if they lived in the United States rather than in orphanages in the United Kingdom or as unwelcome additions to British homes.

A particularly difficult situation, however, entailed the illegitimate offspring of liaisons between African American troops and British women. The dilemma for the British government regarding mixed-race children was that these children were usually unwanted by their mothers in Britain and at the same time the British government was well aware of the racial prejudice that existed in the United States. Was it better to keep the children in Britain, although many were in orphanages, or send them to a country where any trace of African heritage meant denial of basic human rights? In December 1945 the British government estimated there were 550 or more mixed-race children in the United Kingdom and "most of them were in institutions, having been deserted or handed over by their mother." British authorities admitted that abandoned children of African American heritage did not enjoy a promising future in Great Britain; but "the appalling discrimination made in many parts of the U.S. against coloured people [made it] doubt[ful] if the children in question could be made happier by sending them there."[26] A high percentage of these abandoned children came from married women who had affairs with black American GIs, and often the cases did not have the father's name on record or the father had not returned correspondence when notified of the child's birth.

There were also legal barriers to the adoption of an illegitimate child, which made the situation more difficult. The Adoption of Children (Regulation) Act of 1939 did not allow overseas adoption of children unless the adoptive parent was "a British subject or relative or guardian."[27] The father of an illegitimate child was not legally a relative. In addition, any child of a married woman was legally legitimate, complicating any attempts at overseas adoption. Finally, unless the American GIs acknowledged paternity, the children were legally British subjects and therefore restricted by immigration laws from freely entering the United States. Despite these barriers, some illegitimate children did make it to the United States for adoption by their fathers or their fathers' families. Unfortunately, the number of such cases is unknown and the scanty information available in the archival record is inadequate for making estimates. Clearly, some children did make the crossing, as witnessed by the American Red Cross's concern with staying out of the child escort service.

Beyond the statistics, however, is the question of the impact of individual cases of illegitimacy on the participants, black or white. British mothers who were unwed or who were married but had children by men other than their husbands had behaved in a manner that went against the social mores of pre-1939 British society. The postwar return to a more restrictive sexual behavior code highlighted the wartime "indiscretions" of British women with illegitimate children. Neighbors could forget transgressions as long as visual proof of the sin was not evident. Women frequently sent illegitimate children, especially those with black fathers, to orphanages, in part to get beyond the stigma of previous promiscuity. British society had been somewhat tolerant during the war, but the outbreak of peace reversed this trend.[28]

As for the fathers, the scope of their role in the aftermath of illegitimate birth is unclear but raises several questions. How many men who fathered illegitimate children with British women knew of the pregnancy or birth of the child? How many proposed marriage or adoption and were refused? How many GIs ran away from the responsibility and never provided support for the child or the mother? How many paid child maintenance through the years or chose to adopt their offspring? The answers to most of these questions will remain unknown.

Some men clearly were involved in the issue of illegitimacy. Parental pleas for illegitimate children went both ways across the Atlantic. One black GI father, having returned to Atlanta, Georgia, wrote to a Somerset orphanage with an

apeal [sic] for information concerning my daughter Susan which is, or was in your charge there. . . . Susan's mother is the Mrs. _____ of Templecombe, Som. or rather formly [sic] of that address. I received a letter from her stating that she and her husband had gone back with each other and was moving from Templecombe also not to write her any more or to have an allotment made out to her for Susan. But I had already had an allotment made out to her for the purpose of paying you all the fee for Susan's keeps. . . . I've been kind of undecided of what to do. You see more than anything else in the world I want Susan here in America with me and my mother. And all we want to know is how do we go about getting her to the U.S.A. . . . most of all please answer at once of Susan's conditions. I haven't had any news of her since I left France. Mrs. _____ has given me a written statement giving all rights of the child to me and my mother. And mother is just dying to care for the little precious one. . . . Whatever the circumstances are I shall do my best to gain courtesy of the child. I don't want her in an orphan home. She's mine and I want her and my mother wants her. So I shall be all eyes and ears looking and hoping to hear from you. This is a whole hearted request. Please do not fail me. So for now I'll say Cheerio from a Mister.[29]

As this poignant letter illustrates, not every GI father was insensitive and uninvolved in the care of his illegitimate child. In addition, some British women refused offers of marriage from GIs because they did not wish to immigrate to America. Other GIs met their financial obligations willingly and sent support payments on a regular basis. Nonetheless, it is possible to make a strong case that in the majority of instances British women handled pregnancy and the birth of illegitimate or extramarital children on their own.

THE UNFINISHED JOURNEY

A final issue in the catalog of problems that arose for British war brides was "incomplete immigration." This term refers to war brides who do not fit into the immigration story because they either received divorce papers upon their arrival in the United States or decided shortly after they landed that marriage and immigration had been a bad idea. The American government required that someone in the United States accept financial responsibility for emigrating war brides before they left Britain. Hence, in theory, problems resulting from an unfriendly welcome should not have existed. Unfortunately, some British women who arrived in America discovered they had no place to go. As early as 1944, the American Red Cross was handling cases of war brides who, having arrived in the United States, were unwanted by either their husbands or their husbands' families. If the war bride was unwelcome then the American Red Cross could see "no alternative other than referring the bride to the Department of Immigration and Naturalization for return to her place of former residence."[30] If the serviceman was still overseas, the American Red Cross tried to reach the bride's family through the International Red Cross to determine if they could help get the woman back home. If this failed, the Red Cross contacted the Department of Immigration and Naturalization.

By early 1945, the American Red Cross had realistically identified the pitfalls of unsuccessful war bride immigration. Any "unclaimed" war bride arriving in the United States, or any woman who wanted to return home upon arrival, was on her own. Neither the army nor navy had made provisions to return war brides and "government transport service [was] not available under any circumstances."[31] It was up to the war bride or her relatives to finance her return trip; the American Red Cross would not advance funds for this purpose. The Red Cross noted that the United States Immigration laws (Section 75 of the Immigration Act 1917) provided for return transportation of immigrants who became "public charges" but resorting to this method of transportation meant that the immigrant could never return to the United States. Furthermore, children of a marriage to a United States citizen were citizens themselves and did not fall under the provisions of this act. Hence any war bride who contemplated resorting to deportation to gain return passage to Britain had to consider the impact on her children. In addition, the act did not provide financial help in the interim between deciding to return and securing passage; the war bride had to survive on her own.

The only alternative suggested by the American Red Cross was that war brides could petition their own government through the offices of the British embassy and consul to request aid in securing return passage to the United Kingdom. This method of return would not jeopardize a woman's chances of returning to the United States at some future date.[32] Unfortunately, the British government did not want to assume responsibility for distressed war brides either. British authorities believed it would be unfair to treat the war brides differently from any other British subject in the United States. The British consulate in St. Louis, before receiving an official policy statement from the Foreign Office, "informed these women that we have no funds with which to provide their passages and that repatriation at Public expense can only be granted in most exceptional circumstances."[33] The British government's best advice to the war brides was either to earn the money for passage themselves or to rely on relatives or husbands to pay for transportation.

The British embassy informed the Foreign Office of estimates of an 85 percent failure rate for overseas marriages between British women and American GIs. Anticipating a flood of requests for repatriation assistance, the British embassy struggled to form a coherent policy. Officials based their decision to withhold financial help on the assumption "that most victims of these broken marriages would have sufficient resources to pay their own fares back to England, or that the husbands would be glad to be rid of them at this price."[34] Unfortunately, very few women had the necessary finances, which was part of the reason some had taken free government transportation to the United States in the first place.

While most British authorities did not sympathize with the women in these cases, consular and embassy personnel recognized the seriousness of the situation of distressed war brides. They noted that some women "have been given a misleading impression of the sort of home and standard of life which their American husbands would be able to maintain," while others were just unable to adapt to life in a foreign country.[35] The British government's concern was that British women who returned to the United Kingdom, especially by deportation, would jeopardize future options. An additional concern was the awkward legal position of any offspring of these marriages after the repatriation of the mother to Great Britain. Nevertheless, British authorities ultimately placed responsibility for the repatriation of these female immigrants with the individual or the United States government. The British Treasury informed the Foreign Office that "wherever possible, the cost should be allowed to fall on the U.S. government. In choosing to make their lives in the U.S. these women accepted the advantages or disadvantages of living under the laws and regulations prevailing there and willingly sacrificed conditions in the U.K. for conditions unknown to them."[36] In this view, it was not up to the British government to cover the costs of returning British subjects who had made the mistake of marrying a foreigner and emigrating. Some distressed war brides eventually returned to Britain at the expense of the British government. The majority of the women who returned to Britain, however, relied on funds provided by family members.

The biggest concern of British authorities was making sure that British women who wished to return to Great Britain did not do so with such haste that they would have larger problems later. The British government already knew that women who returned to Great Britain before divorcing their husbands would face difficulties. Trying to conduct divorce proceedings against an American from the British side of the Atlantic would be costly if not impossible, as had been proven in the case of British war brides still resident in Britain. In addition, as mentioned earlier, a British woman who married a foreigner and then immigrated and lived with him was not eligible to apply for divorce using the provisions of the Matrimonial Causes (War Marriages) Act of 1944. It was possible for a woman who had not lived with her husband in the United States to proceed with divorce action under this legislation, but this technicality would apply to few women.[37]

The British government advised war brides to remain in the United States long enough to initiate and follow through on divorce proceedings. English law recognized the husband's "domicile" as the controlling factor in divorce proceedings. Authorities advised women that "in order for the decree of divorce to be recognized in England, the British wife should obtain a decree of divorce in the court of the state in the United States where her husband is domiciled, or in a court the validity of whose decrees is recognized by the court of the husbands domicile."[38] The fundamental problem for British women in this situation was financial. The British government initially refused to give financial assistance to British women in the United States who initiated divorce proceedings. Aid open to women in Britain under the Poor Persons Procedure did not apply to women overseas. British authorities argued against giving assistance by stressing that this type of financial aid went beyond any previous help given by the British government to distressed citizens abroad. The British government eventually relented and supplied some financial help in cases where "after full investigation of all the facts of a case it appears to the Consular officer that such action is essential . . . to prevent them becoming or remaining a charge on public funds as distressed British subjects."[39] The British government required British women to repay the funds, however.

A number of war brides fit into this category of women who traveled to the United States but then returned to Britain either immediately or by December 1948, when the War Brides Act expired. A variety of reasons existed for this "incomplete immigration." Most commonly, some war brides made it to the United States but then left within a short time because of homesickness. Several war brides mentioned that on the expedition from their homes through processing at Tidworth and on the ships to New York they observed war brides with severe cases of homesickness. Peggy Virden recalled that when her ship docked in New York several women refused to get off and demanded that they be returned to Britain as quickly as possible.[40] For other women, a hasty retreat to Britain was due to discovery that their husbands no longer wanted them. Sometimes their husbands had initiated divorce proceedings or their in-laws refused to vouch for their support. Some war brides left the United States after only a brief stay when they realized that life in the United States or their husbands' circumstances did not fit with their expectations. Women reunited with husbands could feel overwhelmed when the romance of the courtship and wedding was replaced by the reality of marriage to a foreigner in a foreign land.

How many women returned to Britain soon after immigrating? This is another area of the war bride story with little documentary evidence. In November 1946, the British embassy estimated that approximately five hundred British women needed legal assistance. This figure does not include women who were using their own funds for court procedures or who had already returned to England.[41] The English-Speaking Union, another source of contact for the war brides in the United States, often used the statistic that 5 percent of the marriages were failing.[42] This rate would equate to approximately thirty-five hundred failed marriages in the early days of immigration among the seventy thousand marriages contracted.

Regardless of the exact figures, the number of problem cases was comparatively small. Some divorces between British women and American GIs occurred for the same reasons other wartime marriages failed, such as incompatibility. The marriages took place during the war at a time of heightened emotional tension. Both GIs and war brides initiated divorces in these cases. A reason for failed marriages perhaps more relevant to the story of transatlantic marriage, however, could be a fear of the consequences of the marriages. How many GIs regretted their decision to marry a foreign woman and, hence, initiated divorce proceedings? How many British women married Americans and then decided that emigration was too high a price to pay for marriage to a foreigner? How many children did these failed relationships affect? While the statistics are unknown there is at least one certainty. British women were left alone to face many of these problems. While the governments of the United States and Great Britain often denied responsibility and some GIs evaded it, the women could not.

This idea of "incomplete immigration" differs from other immigration issues. Historians often describe the movement of immigrants back to their homelands as "return migration," a phrase that suggests an economic and/or a temporal dimension in terms of employment and length of stay. It could imply either success or failure. "Incomplete immigration" refers to a decision to return home *before* attempting to live as an immigrant, *before* beginning the adventure. It implies only failure. It is a term that does not apply to the vast majority of war brides who made the trip across the Atlantic and to their husbands' homes. It is in the accounts of women who stayed in America that the story of the immigrant experience lies.

7

Transitions

I just believed everything my husband told me and, of course, a lot of it was kidding. He told me there were no electric lights and they had to use oil lamps. I believed it because there were a lot of girls on board that boat that thought they were going to go to mansions with swimming pools and all that. You know my husband never gave me a false impression; if anything, he went the other way.

—Peggy Virden

The immigration story of British war brides illustrates many of the complexities of assimilation. In the present study, the first stage of the process is termed cultural assimilation, which pertains to the outward signs of conforming to the dominant culture.[1] Several factors influence this process. Immigrant expectations can have an impact on the assimilation process, as can the gender of the immigrant. For British war brides, the transition was, theoretically, eased by a friendly and public welcome in America. They had had the benefit of numerous orientation programs. They were also targeted by various agencies for inclusion in war bride clubs and other organizations in the United States. Interestingly, sponsored orientations and clubs often emphasized the war brides' roles as wives. The war brides themselves, however, founded their own clubs, which were related to their national heritage and not their gender. The fact that they were female was secondary to their cultural identity, although their story is complicated by their immigration to America as wives of United States citizens. The development of contacts among British war brides stresses the persistence of cultural identity and the individuality of immigrant responses to the immigration process. For many British war brides, as for other immigrants, assimilation to American life began with a conception of the United States that they possessed before leaving their homeland. As they confronted the disparities between the myth and the reality of life in America, they uncovered unanticipated problems in adjustment.

British war brides arriving in the United States had an image of life in America garnered from a variety of sources, including their husbands' stories. Some war brides had read books and learned about the United States in school but many more had drawn their ideas from Hollywood. Lack of knowledge or knowledge gained from sources such as Hollywood meant that many war brides had unrealistic expectations about American life. Several agencies recognized the inadequacy of war brides' perceptions of the United States and attempted to correct the problem. Gaining accurate information about America had begun for some war brides in numerous Red Cross clubs in Britain during the war. The American Red Cross Club at Rainbow Corner in London began one of the first war bride orientation classes, which grew out of a Christmas gathering for GIs and their British wives in December 1943. The American Red Cross officials decided to hold monthly classes because the women had inundated them with questions. The nature of these questions led Red Cross personnel to recognize a need to "de-glamorize" the women's view of America. The program director noted that they wanted "to bridge the gap between what Hollywood shows America to be like, and what these women will really find when they get there."[2]

Some British women apparently did believe their lives in America would be glamorous. June Porter remembered the influence of Hollywood. She imagined her life in America based on "the movies, with priscilla curtains. I thought that was what I was coming to. White priscilla curtains, the whole thing, white fence. We all had that picture, I think."[3] To correct these images, the Red Cross classes at Rainbow Corner included lectures on American culture and discussions of topics such as the American education system, small-town community life, fashion, and the types of women's clubs the war brides could eventually join to meet and get to know American women. On occasion, guest speakers such as Mrs. Edward R. Murrow, Adele Astaire, and Eleanor Roosevelt appeared. Sometimes, however, speakers went further than offering practical tips and ventured into critiques of American culture. At one meeting, Helen Kirkpatrick, a *Chicago Daily News* reporter, advised the brides that "American men are very protective, but they expect a lot of their wives. The clinging vine is wonderful in the pre-marriage stages, but thereafter she has to be strong enough to take it."[4] Kirkpatrick was, of course, addressing her comments to women who were war "veterans" by 1944. Often the people delivering advice were as unenlightened about war brides as the war brides were of life in America.

While orientations focusing on topics such as current women's fashion might seem trivial, this type of preview of life in the United States was helpful. Practical tips on clothes and manners could form the foundation of cultural assimilation. Newly arriving immigrants are often eager to blend in quickly, and British war brides had some legitimate concerns about this. Years of rationing meant the average war bride's wardrobe was out of date. Peggy Virden remembered with embarrassment her arrival in New York. She recalled that, while waiting outside a theater before attending a performance by Carmen Miranda, "we got lots of stares from people in the street.... I suppose we looked like a lot of frumps, you know, flat-heeled shoes and boots, tweed suits."[5] The opinion of strangers was not the sole concern of war brides upon their arrival in America, however. They also had in-laws to impress. Hence, in December 1944, British war brides in London would have been glad to learn that American women wore "simple cotton dresses."

When Eleanor Roosevelt spoke to the war brides in January 1946 she gave practical tips as well as thought-provoking advice. Her comments at Rainbow Corner addressed some of the basic issues of immigrant assimilation. Mrs. Roosevelt suggested that war brides would need a great deal of patience and understanding when dealing with Americans. She observed that the average American would not comprehend the wartime experiences of the brides and that they believed America's wartime ordeal had been difficult. Mrs. Roosevelt pointed out that American and British cultures differed in some basic ways by referring to the British tradition of afternoon tea. Far more seriously, Mrs. Roosevelt warned the brides that in some areas of the United States there was "perfectly unreasonable prejudice" that might tax the patience of the immigrating brides. She advised that this prejudice might even include misperceptions of the British. Further, Mrs. Roosevelt noted that many Americans had seen the publicity about war brides' taking shipping space away from returning GIs and she advised the brides to have a ready answer if confronted with this issue. She also reminded the women that the United States was experiencing a severe housing shortage and that they should be prepared for this problem when they arrived.[6]

The war bride orientation classes spread from Rainbow Corner to most other Red Cross clubs in Britain and, eventually, to France, Italy, Germany, and other European countries. The British project led the way and eventually officials there issued suggestions for other clubs, including the use of "maps, pamphlets, films and lectures to convey information about American history, geography, government and literature . . . [and] matters of practical and immediate importance, such as monetary conversion tables, measurements used in American recipes, how to use an American pullman, the words to the *Star Spangled Banner,* and how to pledge allegiance to the flag."[7] The classes in Europe often included English-language instruction. The American Red Cross summed up its "schools for wives" by noting that the overall motivation of most women who attended was that "they want very much not to be different and to be accepted and understood, especially by 'his' family."[8] The desire not to be "different" suggests that cultural assimilation had begun for some British war brides through these Red Cross programs.

Unfortunately, the Red Cross club orientations could not reach all war brides in Britain. However, similar orientation classes occurred on board the bride ships to America. The American Red Cross and the army transportation officers on board conducted daily lectures throughout the voyage on many of the ships. The sessions covered a variety of practical issues including how the political process worked in the United States and how to get citizenship. Lecturers spoke on the physical features of different states, types of American food, availability of medical services, and the exact procedure to follow when the ship docked. One Red Cross worker noted that the war brides were eager "to make a genuine success of their new life."[9] While the Red Cross classes in Britain were available only to war brides within reasonable distance, the shipboard classes could, theoretically, reach all war brides. However, the American Red Cross reported that attendance at orientation lectures on board ships was not heavy. By comparison, other activities such as the nightly movie always drew capacity crowds. Nevertheless, those who did attend lectures perhaps came away with a better understanding of their new homes.

War brides could also benefit from the advice of British women who had made the trip to the United States before the bulk of the crossings in 1946. Articles ran in service magazines and local British papers describing the friendly reception and minor differences the first war brides encountered. Small things like door locks and screen doors baffled the new arrivals, while other brides found it would take a while to get used to ambulance sirens after the air raids in Britain. Most war brides would not know their own sizes when it came time to shop for clothes and would often have to learn new terms for old standbys; what the British called "roll-ons" the Americans knew as girdles. Americans also kept windows closed, advised one early war bride, but tea was available in the United States. According to one woman, the predeparture information most war brides received about New York from numerous sources was not sufficient. "It's more beautiful, more rushing, more everything than anyone can describe," she said.[10] This reaction was shared by war brides who settled in many other areas of the United States.

Early war brides, who garnered a great deal of publicity, often told reporters that they had anticipated some aspects of life in America. All the women had, by virtue of their marriages, learned some American slang and habits. Many had worked with GIs throughout the war, prompting one woman to claim she "had learned what to expect— even the Brooklyn accent."[11] Another woman admitted that her husband had destroyed any illusions about life in America by letting her know it "was just like any other place, a little better maybe, but nothing like what Hollywood made out."[12]

The British *Good Housekeeping Magazine* and the United States Office of War Information published an eighteen-page pamphlet entitled *A Bride's Guide to the U.S.A.*, which was another source of information on America available to the British war brides. As with the orientation classes, the pamphlet included both practical guidelines and a discussion of American culture. The appendixes offered information on currency conversion, a glossary of American and British terms, necessary travel procedures and paperwork for war brides, and a suggested list of books on American life.[13]

The book list included both fictional and historical accounts of general life in the United States as well as regional treatments. Interestingly, since no distinction was made between fiction and nonfiction, some novels, such as *Gone with the Wind* by Margaret Mitchell and *The Virginian* by Owen Wister, could only add to the misunderstandings of newly arriving immigrants. Unless the readers were well versed in changes in American history and culture by 1946, they could conceivably believe that *The Virginian* described contemporary "western cattle country" in America. Nonfiction on the reading list included more academic fare such as Margaret Mead's *The American Culture* and J. C. Furnas's *How America Lives*. Although these books were more descriptive of actual conditions in the United States, they were less likely to have been read than the popular literature. The guide suggested that war brides could learn about America when they arrived by visiting a local library. War brides, according to the pamphlet, would gain help in adjusting to life in America from reading "novels about your state and region." In addition, it advised war brides to subscribe to both a local paper and a woman's magazine to keep up with current news and fashions.

The bulk of the guide gave advice for easing adjustment to life in America. The pamphlet was similar to the GI guide to Great Britain that the army gave to men as they headed to the United Kingdom. The bride's guide defined the cultural differences between Britain and the United States with tips on American humor, shyness, manners, small towns, big cities, and homemaking. It explained that Americans were basically shy but covered it up well. It admonished war brides to open up to people they met as much as possible. The guide warned the brides about the American sense of humor by reminding them that "exaggeration, of course, you know about . . . kidding is perhaps harder to get used to, but you have to learn." Americans used kidding to test a person, the authors declared, so the war brides needed to be tough and take it and, even better, learn to laugh at themselves. The guide also cautioned the brides to refrain from trying to "kid back" until they had a firm understanding of how the system worked.

Small-town life, according to the guide, meant the war brides would need to learn the art of "neighbourliness." This included talking to neighbors, arranging an evening's entertaining at one's home, and participating in informal drop-in visiting. Circumstances would be different in the city. Neighborliness was not a part of big-city life, according to the guide, which meant that new arrivals would have to use other methods to get to know strangers. The best way to go about this was to join a club or organization such as the church, the Young Women's Christian Association (YWCA), the Red Cross, or hobby groups. The guide informed the brides that get-togethers with friends were far more formal in the city than in the rural areas; few people just "dropped in."

The pamphlet went on to tutor the British war brides in what to expect concerning American philosophies toward life. Americans did not "settle down" like people in Great Britain. Instead, Americans were far more likely to be on the move both physically and socially; "this mobile life may make you homesick. . . . Anyhow, you may as well like it, for this is the way of life that has built the British Commonwealth of Nations as well as the United States." The advice to brides explained that one of the best ways for them to contribute to economic mobility was to be good homemakers. The guide provided information on typical salaries and household budgets. Although the pamphlet suggested that no one would criticize the war brides for seeking employment outside the home, it also informed the women that their "main job . . . will be running the house." The guide advised the war brides not to overspend; American companies targeted housewives when they advertised their goods, so the war brides should learn to be very discerning. Concurrently, the guide warned the women to hold off on expanding their wardrobes until they knew exactly what the climate would be in their new homes. Other tips included a short discussion of American meals and food preparation using canned goods, the prevalence of central heating throughout America, and the importance of keeping a simple but good-quality wardrobe that avoided "bows, 'froo-froos,' and tricky cuts."

Surprisingly, the bride's guide also included a section on nativism in the United States. The authors admitted that while Americans acknowledged settlement of the United States by immigrants, there were still groups of people who were disliked throughout the country. In some areas, the pamphlet advised, war brides would discover prejudice against any number of ethnic and cultural minorities, including African Americans, Jews, Catholics, and Japanese. In some cases, it warned, the war brides might even meet people who disliked the British. The guide went on to point out that a number of immigrant groups in the United States were not completely "Americanized." More optimistically, however, the war brides would find that Americans were willing to accept most anyone who would work hard and who was courageous enough to immigrate. The booklet went on to explain that "except for a few girls who have connections in America already, most British brides arrive entirely unknown. No one knows who you were at home, and in most places no one cares very much to dig into your past. Practically no Americans are able to 'place' you by your accent. It is what you are that is important. If they like you, they like you, and if they don't like you, a good address in London is no help. This, in fact, is what most Americans went to America for—a fresh start with no questions asked."[14]

While the scope of advice to the war brides contained in the guide was impressive, the underlying themes and assumptions were single-minded. One clear message was that war brides would find their lives in America centered in the domestic sphere, hence the tips on food preparation, running the household, and neighborly behavior. When the Office of War Information prepared the guide, it obviously felt that enlisting the aid of the British *Good Housekeeping Magazine,* a publication devoted entirely to a female audience and well-versed in women's issues, was the best way to reinforce the notion of the ideal role of women. Who better to define a woman's place in American society now that the war was over and everyone could go back to their traditional roles? Married women in full-time, paid work had been useful in wartime but now it was time for women to go back to "running the house."

The second theme of the guide was to enlighten readers regarding American culture and prejudice. The explanation that immigrants were free to make their way in America reinforced the myth of the melting pot. A more subtle message within this immigrant portrait specifically targeted the war brides. By assuring them that their accents were anonymous in America the pamphlet was really suggesting that their social class was unknowable, even noting that "a good address in London is no help." It is doubtful that the targets of this advice were British women from good addresses. More likely, the issue of questionable character that had plagued many of the war brides, from their association with GIs in their hometowns through the army transportation system, had found its way into the literature. The question for the British war brides was, What image did Americans have of them? Did Americans believe, as did a number of British subjects, that "war bride" was another term for a woman who had fooled around and hooked an American to better her standard of living through free immigration to the United States? Obviously, these women faced numerous challenges associated with their status as immigrants and war brides.

Most British war brides were anxious about their reception in the United States, especially that first reunion with their husbands and their introduction to their new in-laws. For many war brides these first few weeks were critical for their adjustment to their new home. The process of immigration was over but the process of assimilation was just beginning. Many brides recall those first few days as whirlwinds of hectic activity and new experiences. Some remember being amazed at the quantity and variety of food available at local markets. Clothes were also more accessible than in England and could be acquired without ration cards. Often it was the everyday things that seemed the most strange. Peggy Virden, who arrived in Iowa after her long journey, remembered getting

> my first bath, good bath, in about eight or ten days . . . and then we went down to Kellerton and, of course, they were all there. We had a big family dinner that night when we got down there, Grandma had fixed it. . . . My mother always used to do everything on a plate for us, it was all dished and that was what you got, but they had everything in bowls. They passed the bowls around and when they passed that bowl of corn I didn't eat it. I said, "Oh, I'm not going to eat that. It's maize, my mother feeds that to the chickens."[15]

Sybil Afdem commented on the difference in types of housing and described her first home as "a little house with wooden floors, and it didn't have any fireplaces. It had one of those wood stoves right in the living room with a big pipe . . . and the upstairs was kind of unfinished. . . . I remember thinking, if my mother could see me, if mother and dad could see me."[16]

The majority of war brides received a friendly welcome from in-laws and other Americans. Some women had already been in contact with their husband's family by mail, which helped ease the initial tension. For most brides, however, that first week in America was a mind-numbing round of meeting many strangers who were actually their new family. Margaret Wharton noted that when she first arrived, "I was regarded as something of an oddity, with my pronounced accent and typically English looks. Friends and relatives were very kind and hospitable, trades people were helpful. . . . I was interviewed by newspaper reporters . . . and was generally made much of. It was all quite exciting and gratifying but of course it was a short-lived phase that already had begun to pall. I was then faced with the task of getting down to daily life in a strange country with little money to spend and many lonely hours to face."[17]

Indeed this novelty did wear off but often not before the war brides had experienced fleeting fame, which could come in the form of newspaper articles and dockside receptions or more formal welcomes from local community leaders and dignitaries. One such welcome took place in Everett, Washington, on 1 October 1946, for war brides who had emigrated from all over the world. Senator Henry M. Jackson and his staff arranged a reception that consisted of appearances by representatives of state and local government and the British and French consulates; the participation of local veterans groups, chapters of the American Red Cross, newspapers, and radio stations; and an address from General Mark Clark. Jackson had written to President Harry S Truman requesting that the White House send a message to the war brides as part of the welcoming ceremonies. He had noted the list of dignitaries who would be present in addition to "approximately forty-five foreign war brides now residing in this county."[18] Truman's secretary replied that despite Senator Jackson's belief that this reception was unique, there were so many events of this type going on throughout the United States that the President had "not been able to recognize them with individual messages."[19]

The White House response further illustrates that numerous communities arranged some type of welcoming ceremonies for the war brides, an experience not enjoyed by other immigrants in American history. From the first, as foreigners married to Americans overseas, the war brides had been operating out of the mainstream of the immigrant experience. Marriage to a United States citizen, free transatlantic transportation, specific bride ships, and so on, set them apart. The publicity surrounding the arrival of the war brides further established the profound differences between war brides and other immigrant groups. Molly Tagart, a Seattle war bride, recalled that "the *Seattle PI* [*Post Intelligencer*] sent a reporter out because I was the first one here. . . . They took us to a grocery store and they pointed out that what I called a biscuit you called a cookie. They followed us around and had quite a write-up in the *PI*. . . . Then, when our first son was born, they did another write-up and took pictures of him and I in the hospital."[20] Uniquely, the war brides not only arrived in the United States under intense public scrutiny, they also experienced a positive reception from the larger population. It is hard to determine the impact this public welcome had on the assimilation of war brides into American society since many other factors also shaped their experiences. Despite the national reception, however, war brides still faced assimilation problems as did other immigrants, if from a somewhat different perspective and for different reasons.

Part of the problem for arriving war brides was the acute housing shortage in postwar America. Many war brides had to live with strangers upon their arrival. A conference in February 1946 on the housing shortage, attended by representatives of the American Red Cross, attempted to address some of the problems of returning veterans in search of homes. The Red Cross educated its local chapters on veterans' problems and the stress associated with the lack of housing. Most people agreed that ex-servicemen should have priority for housing, both for buying and for renting, but the problem was bigger than simple numbers. People at the time recognized that the housing shortage went back to the 1920s, when the economy played a major role in discouraging new construction. It would be a long time, in most people's estimation, before enough housing existed for all veterans. In addition, the available research suggested that "only 10 percent of veterans can afford a rent of $50 a month and 40 percent cannot afford more than $30 a month." The estimated postwar demand for houses topped three million, and veterans and veterans' organizations believed that ex-servicemen should not be the ones forced to pay the price of the housing shortage and "be compelled to live with their mothers-in-law."[21]

Unlike other married ex-GIs, who might reside with their wives' parents, veterans with foreign-born wives often would have to live with the veteran's parents. For many of the reunited couples this put an

added strain on the wife's immigrant experience. The housing shortage in postwar America was dramatic. Fully 76 percent of the British
war brides in the 1989 survey said that when they began married life
in the United States they lived with other people.[22] It is important to
keep in mind that these couples, some of whom had been married
for three or four years, had never lived together as man and wife.
When the adjustment to married life took place under the scrutiny
of the husband's family, additional problems could develop. Many
British war brides faced openly hostile environments. June Porter,
whose mother-in-law did not like the idea of having a foreign-born
daughter-in-law, remembered her first home in the United States as
"a clean one, a shabby one but it was clean. I have to point that out.
She was a very clean lady but this is where they were living so that's
where I came."[23] Joan Posthuma, who did not have to share housing
with in-laws, still remembers the housing shortage in Dallas, where
she and her husband "lived in one room, which if my mother or my
family had known, they would have been horrified. There were no
places. There was nothing there."[24]

The strain on war brides could intensify if the in-laws in question
were foreign-born themselves. This situation added to problems of
adjustment. Many British war brides were unaware of the multiethnic character of the American population. During the war the American GIs in Britain appeared homogeneous. Military uniforms denot-
ed branch of service, rank, and little else. The American accent was
universally strange despite regional or ethnic variants. Upon arrival
in the United States a war bride might discover that her "American"
husband was of Italian, Polish, or Greek ancestry. Sometimes the
immigrant parents of ex-servicemen did not speak English.

In 1945 *Yank* magazine reported the story of one English woman
whose in-laws were Italian, which added a tremendous burden to her
adjustment. This woman decided to end the marriage after two
months.[25] Another British war bride recalled her introduction to and
subsequent domicile with her Russian-born in-laws as a disaster. According to her memories, her husband usually sided with his parents
in any disputes and she felt like a complete outsider. She experienced
an intense sense of isolation since they all spoke Russian. She confessed that she had no idea that America was such a multiethnic society. Living with foreign-born in-laws added to her culture shock and
she admitted that she would never marry an American and emigrate
if she had her life to live again. She has counseled her daughters to
marry within their own culture. Part of the problem for this particular bride could have been her own admitted naiveté: she was look-

ing for an escape from war-ravaged Britain and had a "Hollywood" image of the United States. She stayed in the United States but revealed that she was an orphan, so she had no one to go back to in Britain, which made her choice easier.[26]

The ethnic backgrounds of American GIs who participated in the 1989 survey reflect the immigration history of the United States. The majority came from Britain, Ireland, Germany, and Scandinavia. Interestingly, 26 percent of the American GI husbands had immigrant parents, which meant that potentially one quarter of the British war brides could expect to have in-laws who were immigrants themselves.[27] Half of these recent immigrants were from areas of southern and central Europe. The war brides had a wide range of experiences relative to ethnicity in America. Ivy Hammer's mother-in-law in Detroit "didn't speak English, which made it kind of difficult, and at that time we lived in a Polish neighborhood, a very nice neighborhood, very nice. In the shops they all spoke Polish. . . . It was terrible not to speak English . . . going shopping, I found it very difficult, very, very difficult."[28] This war bride eventually became ill from the stress. A member of the English-Speaking Union reported the case of another British war bride "whose husband is the youngest of eight and whose Polish parents speak no English—all the seven brothers and sisters are married to Polish-speaking Americans and some of them and their children live in the same house with their parents—as does Mrs. M. and her baby. There is a resentment against the newcomers and they all speak Polish together. . . she was on the verge of a nervous breakdown."[29]

Not all war bride problems were as dramatic as these, but the potential problems of multiethnic households existed for approximately a quarter of the women. An additional consideration is the case of war brides who married into nonimmigrant families in the United States but who lived in ethnic neighborhoods. The issue of race arose, which many war brides had difficulty understanding. Joan Posthuma, who ended up in Dallas, described her husband's grandmother as "brash, always talking about niggers and things, something that we never heard of. . . . I remember when I met her I was absolutely horrified. I didn't understand this. Everybody was the same, I had been brought up to believe."[30] The war brides had to adjust to America's racism as well as its cultural pluralism. The process must have been even more difficult considering the homogeneous nature of British society in 1945.

While British war brides mentioned religious differences with their spouses as a problem in a few cases, most did not. Perhaps couples had more pressing problems to confront. More likely, difficulties did not occur because British war brides and American GIs were overwhelmingly Protestant. The numbers of brides and GIs in the 1989 survey who were Jewish were almost even. However, the biggest religious difference among couples pertained to membership in the Catholic church; more than twice as many GIs as war brides were Catholic.[31] The difference between the number of Catholic husbands and Catholic wives suggests that religion was an issue that had the potential to be a problem. Molly Tagart, a Catholic war bride with a Protestant husband, recalled that their religious differences did not cause a conflict at first. Her children were baptized Catholic and, she said, "we would go to church and daddy would go to church. Then one day they said, 'Why won't daddy come to church with us?' Well, its not worth it. So we switched. We go to the Methodist Church . . . because it was affecting the family life."[32]

The one area that war brides most frequently identified as a problem was their relations with their in-laws. Conflict often arose due to the simple fact that the son had married a foreign woman. One mother-in-law, quoted in *Yank*, recalled that her "son was engaged to a girl he had gone through school with. They had the same interests, and she's a beautiful, intelligent girl. They had great plans. . . . But then, while he was overseas, this happened."[33] Certainly, resentful in-laws did play a part in the adjustment of war brides to their new homes. Some women recalled in-laws who were mean, drunken, or indifferent. These women fought an extra battle in the struggle to adapt to life in the United States. Fortunately, for the majority of British war brides, their in-laws were more welcoming and helpful. The results of the 1989 survey given in table 3 reflect war bride responses to the issue of reception in America. The overall response of Americans was favorable toward the women. British war brides benefited, as immigrants, from an acceptance in the United States.

The British perhaps fared better than non–English-speaking war brides. A nationwide poll in 1944 about which peoples the United States should allow to immigrate revealed the advantage of being a British subject. The British topped the list of preferred foreigners, followed by Swedes and Russians, although it is worth noting that one-quarter of those polled said immigration of the British to America should stop.[34] The responses of British war brides to the question of discrimination, in the 1989 survey, followed the same pattern. The overwhelming majority of British war brides said that they did not experience any discrimination in the United States. Approximately one-fifth, however, noted a definite prejudice from a variety of indi-

Table 3. War Bride Reception

	In-laws	GI Relatives	GI Friends	Other
Excellent	60%	62%	63%	39%
Good	24	24	30	47
Fair	10	13	6	12
Poor	6	1	1	3

viduals such as their in-laws, husband's friends, employers, neighbors, and strangers. The prejudice some people displayed toward the war brides could often have to do with the question of personality and/or conduct as well. As Ivy Hammers put it: "I had another stripe against me too in those days. I smoked and I wasn't averse to having a drink either. Well, of course, that was terrible. His mother thought I was a tart, I am sure."[35] June Porter recalled, "I only ever met one person who was very nasty, besides my mother-in-law, a young woman. We had gone to a picnic . . . maybe a month after I had been here. . . . I was a thin person and she was, when I look back, she was single and she was plump. . . . She was very rude to me and she made a remark about, 'Well, they said they didn't feed you in England.' She was just mean."[36]

Faced with a myriad of adjustment problems, what did British war brides do? Some typical coping mechanisms used by immigrants and identified by researchers in immigration history include involvement with the church, reading native-language newspapers, and joining ethnic clubs. For immigrants these mechanisms could provide both a means of maintaining ethnic identity within a foreign environment and a means of promoting assimilation. Immigrant religious participation has taken many forms, from membership in an established denomination to creation of separate sects.

Since the Episcopal church was well established in the United States, British war brides had a clear link to their native faith. However, they did not identify the Episcopal church as playing a major part in their adjustment to life in America. Some noted that they met other British war brides through the church, but this method of contact involved few. Most British war bride interviewees felt that the church did not play a large role in their lives before immigration or after. Rosa Ebsary recalled that, although she went to the local Episcopal church in America for many years, her family left for a while because "there was so much commotion with the Vietnamese war and changing the prayer book and throwing out all the things that we believed in that it made us more upset going to church than not going so we finally withdrew our pledge. . . . I think it was very hard for me adjusting to the commercial approach of the church."[37] The Episcopal church seemed foreign to some British war brides. Many women found it easier to attend their husbands' churches. The lack of involvement with the church in the United States is not surprising since religious participation in Great Britain in the 1940s was remarkably low. British war brides were not coming from an actively religious culture.

The question of native-language newspapers does not apply to British war brides. As English-speakers, British immigrants did not face the additional trauma of arriving in a country where they could not read the native language or understand native speakers. This is no doubt the reason that historians have traditionally glossed over the question of British immigrants' assimilation into American society. Certainly British war brides' responses to the 1989 survey question about language bear out these findings. Only 10 percent cited a language problem and most said that this usually took the form of misunderstandings or ridicule. Occasionally the language issue, as noted earlier, had to do with ethnic neighbors. While some newspaper stories had assured the war brides that their "English" accents would be welcome in the United States, other publications, such as the guide, provided a glossary of terms so war brides would be able to understand American English.

British war brides were not subject to the isolation that non–English-speaking immigrants endured. However, they spoke with an accent that often set them apart from a society into which they were trying to blend. All British war brides had a foreign accent from the American perspective and each woman encountered comments of one form or another. The level of awareness about accents and pronunciation varied in the United States. For instance, some war brides mentioned problems with specific words such as "privacy" while one British woman recalled that "some people were surprised I spoke such good English, others wanted to know which side I was on" in the war.[38] Other war brides believed that the issue of speech was problematic and recalled their efforts to lose traces of their accents. This effort to conform often was fostered by their new American relatives and friends. In June 1945 an American GI in Britain introduced his war bride to his parents back home over the telephone and pointed out his wife's accent. He suggested that "we'll see that she gets rid of that when we get her home won't we."[39] Conversely, many British war brides recalled instances when people asked them to speak. One woman said, "I was asked repeatedly to repeat what I said. Then I found out it was just to hear my voice."[40] So, while language may not have been a barrier to communication for British war brides, the women's accents did set them apart as foreigners in postwar America. Ivy Hammers recalled that while living in Detroit she was traveling by streetcar to the International Institute "on a street called 'Du Bois.' Well, when I saw it I asked the streetcar man to put me off at 'Dubois.' He said, 'Ya mean de boys.' Oh, all these things, it was like being slapped in the face with a kipper."[41] Just how "foreign" the war brides felt as a result of their accents is hard to determine, but there can be no doubt that their accents set them apart. Although their accents have diminished over time, some traces are still present fifty years after the women arrived in the United States. The war brides still are asked their nationality; however, people usually suspect they are Canadian or Australian.

A third method historians have suggested immigrants use to assist in assimilation is membership in ethnic clubs and organizations. These organizations take various forms and fill a variety of functions, from religious to social. Oscar Handlin observed that since immigrants could not completely recreate old communities, they found ways of replacing them in their new environment. The formation of clubs was one such method. These organizations were incredibly durable, according to Handlin, and many continued after the immigrants who founded them were gone. In his discussion of clubs among other ethnic groups, he noted that "analogous organizations developed among the British."[42] These clubs and organizations often filled a void in immigrants' lives. For instance, in the nineteenth century many organizations carried on welfare functions that have since been addressed by the government. Social and cultural organizations, however, have a different function, which directly relates to the bonds of ethnicity.

For British war brides the establishment of clubs and organizations took on special significance. Unlike earlier immigrant groups to the United States, British war brides did not settle into ethnic or national enclaves. As noted earlier, they immigrated not as a national group but rather as a function of their gender. The fact that they were British was secondary to their married status. As a result, British war brides settled all over the United States, wherever their husbands lived. A war bride might discover that she was the only British immigrant in the area, certainly the only one in her neighborhood. Sybil

Afdem recalled that she lived "in a house next to my in-laws for the first seven years I was married and I didn't know anybody. I had no neighbors that I had anything to do with, I had no friends, all I knew was my husband's family and, of course, the two brothers didn't have wives."[43] The isolation could be intense. Like other immigrants before them, British war brides often wanted to talk with other people in similar circumstances.

Many existing agencies and organizations recognized that war brides would need the companionship of other women to ease the loneliness. The first major organization involved in founding British war bride clubs was the English-Speaking Union. The Union was established in 1920 to promote "friendship and understanding among English-speaking people" of the world.[44] When British war brides began arriving in the United States, the English-Speaking Union attempted to address the need for a support group for these new immigrants. Besides helping British war brides who were in distress shortly after their arrival, the Union also established war bride clubs in various branches in cities throughout the United States to help the women adjust to their new lives.

In late 1945 *Stars and Stripes* reported that British war brides in the United States were attending English-Speaking Union clubs. Club publicity hinted that British women would find adjustment to life in America easier by participating in group activities. One woman recalled that she would go "to the one in New York, and drink tea and talk about home with other English girls. And so loneliness goes."[45] By 1946, the English-Speaking Union had managed to set up Overseas Bride Clubs in thirty-five different cities that were open to war brides from any country. These clubs provided a place where war brides could interact with women who were facing the same challenges. The group meetings also allowed the foreign-born women to meet American women, which many people hoped would aid in the immigrants' adjustment to American life. The clubs helped the war brides "in solving a variety of everyday problems—from finding a home or a job to aiding them with shopping, rationing, cooking and budget problems. . . . Typical of the clubrooms is that in New York City. Here, in addition to a lounge, is a kitchenette where brides can brew their own tea, a sewing room with machines on which they can learn to stitch, and—most important—women with whom they can talk."[46]

The English-Speaking Union had worked closely with the American Red Cross to establish a comprehensive approach to war bride problems. The two organizations agreed upon a separation of the services that they would provide to the women. The American Red Cross maintained its program of aiding wives of American servicemen who needed financial help or assistance in applying for allotments and insurance. The Red Cross also continued its function of helping wives communicate with their husbands in the service and of providing minimal "consultation and guidance," usually in the form of referrals, for wives who were experiencing job, child care, or health problems. The American Red Cross, however, was reluctant to aid war brides whose husbands were discharged. As can be seen throughout this study, the organization provided a variety of services to war brides if somewhat reluctantly.

Initially, the English-Speaking Union and the American Red Cross agreed that the English-Speaking Union was in a much better position to provide personal services for the war brides of World War II.[47] The Union began its program to help war brides before the women left Britain. Part of this program took the form of distribution of a pamphlet on Union activities to British war brides at Tidworth Camp, before they boarded their ships. The pamphlet assured the brides that "A Cordial Welcome Awaits You at the English-Speaking Union of the United States" and asked:

> Do you want to learn to cook the American way?
> Do you want to sew?
> Do you know about American money and how far it goes?
> Do you want to meet other wives who have come from your own country, possibly from your own "home town"?
> Do you hope to meet some American girls who can tell you how they do things?
> Do you want a job?
> Do you want help in finding a place to live? (That's a hard one, but we'll try.)
> Do you fear you may ever be homesick? Maybe it would help to talk to someone who has been homesick too and can tell you how to get over it.[48]

The list of activities and functions that the English-Speaking Union promoted suggests various levels of aid to British war brides. Some activities reinforced the brides' duties within the woman's sphere: cooking, sewing, and budget management. The pamphlet also encouraged their development of a female network by mingling with women from both Britain and America. Finally, the English-Speaking Union hoped to provide a means for British war brides to discuss issues of immigration: homesickness and coping mechanisms. It wanted British war brides to adjust to America by understanding that differences between the British and Americans could seem major but really were not. However, the Union strove to make sure that by offering its services it was not in any way promoting the "segregation" of British war brides from the rest of American society. While the English-Speaking Union would provide an atmosphere where women could talk openly about personal problems, including the concerns of the immigrant living in a strange land, it tried not to lose sight of "the ultimate objective of their settling down happily in their various local communities . . . and excessive clannishness is discouraged."[49] The Union pamphlet encouraged British war brides to contact the nearest branch when they arrived in America.

Other groups and organizations also worked to provide facilities for war brides who were struggling to adjust to life in the United States. The Young Women's Christian Association sponsored war bride clubs throughout the United States. Like the English-Speaking Union, YWCA clubs covered a variety of activities for war brides but mainly provided a place where the women could go and interact with other people experiencing similar problems. This was also the aim of the war bride clubs organized in various cities by branches of the American Red Cross. Although it originally left club work to other organizations, the American Red Cross eventually worked in conjunction with the English-Speaking Union because the Red Cross had more local chapters in cities and towns across America. The organization sponsored programs similar to those of the English-Speaking Union and the YWCA. One Red Cross club in Pennsylvania invited a British war bride of World War I to talk to the more recent immigrants and give insight into the problems of adjusting to life in America.[50] These various clubs could often make a difference for war brides who were feeling particularly isolated in their new environment.

Like the English-Speaking Union, the majority of clubs emphasized adjustment to aspects of American society that reinforced gender stereotypes. Cooking, sewing, and homemaking were the foundation of women's lives as envisioned by these organizations. The Americanization of female immigrants in postwar American society meant that they should settle down to the ideal family life. What better way for a group of new immigrants, who had become immigrants because of their marital relationship, to make the transition to American culture than to play their expected role? Hence, banding together in clubs was one method of meeting other homemakers as well as fellow immigrants. Most war brides, however, did not join clubs sponsored by large agencies such as the English-Speaking Union, the American Red

Cross, the YWCA, and the Daughters of the British Empire. The women started their own independent clubs. War brides of all nationalities found each other and organized at the grass roots level, from small midwestern towns to government housing projects near military bases.

The reasons war brides came together are diverse but it is safe to say that their immediate needs had little to do with their concern over homemaking skills. A more important motivation was the desire to interact with people who had shared experiences as immigrant women. For instance, Ivy Hammers, who had become ill due to loneliness, remembered when her husband took her to "the International Institute in Detroit and a very lovely lady was in charge. . . . The different war brides' groups assembled there and we had a lovely club, we used to have parties and bazaars. It saved my life, really. I was very depressed."[51] Joan Posthuma, whose husband stayed in the armed forces, recalled, "When we lived in Alexandria, there were about thirty of us down there. . . . We formed our own club. . . . I don't even remember what we called it. . . . It was wonderful. . . . It did help. We used to have a monthly meeting and we used to do things. Some of us would meet in the park and have picnics. This went on for quite some time. . . . It was something to do, we had somebody to talk to."[52] Having someone to talk to, who understood one's circumstances, could be crucial.

Some local war bride clubs started as one thing and ended up as something completely different. For instance, in February 1947 British war brides in Everett, Washington, founded the International Wives Organization (IWO). The club began when a home economist from Puget Sound Power and Light Company offered cooking lessons to a group of war brides after a civic reception. The women at these lessons decided to form a club. The local chapter of the Veterans of Foreign Wars lent the women a meeting room where they drew up their club's constitution and by-laws. The first meeting was held at the Everett Public Library and was attended by twenty-six foreign-born wives.[53] Membership included any foreign- or American-born wife of a World War II veteran. Though the idea to include American women was admirable, there were never many American-born members. The purpose of the IWO was to promote good fellowship among members and to help in civic projects. The *Everett Herald* ran articles publicizing the founding of the IWO and announcing monthly meetings.

The IWO soon included women from many nations but in the beginning the majority were from the British Commonwealth, with representatives from Great Britain, Australia, and New Zealand predominating. Members contacted possible recruits in a variety of ways. Joyce Osnes, who was not a war bride but was a British immigrant, recalled that two club members "came to see me because I had been to church. It took me a long time to find the Church of England. The minister apparently had met M. so she came on some sort of committee to see me."[54] Over the years the club expanded to include wives of veterans of other wars as well. Members came from all over the world, including Hawaii, the Philippines, Egypt, France, Germany, Italy, Korea, Japan, Turkey, and Chile.

Meetings frequently included talks by members. Some women would describe their homeland, perhaps easing homesickness by talking about the country they had left. Other women gave talks about parts of the United States or other countries they had visited, while one woman's presentation was broadly titled "international affairs." Club projects varied and included giving Christmas packages to needy families in the area as well as sending some to European children. The IWO also sponsored children at Northern State Hospital and the Rainier School in Buckley. Charitable deeds often played a large role in other war bride clubs as well. While the women gathered to help each other, they also pooled their resources to help people and organizations outside their circle. The Everett club provided war brides with much-needed contact outside the home. Sybil Afdem remembered that, before she joined the IWO, the only people she really knew were her husband's family. She recalled that her membership in the IWO was the time when she "started to enjoy girlfriends."[55] The women would meet in the evenings at each other's homes, where refreshments were served and friendships formed.

The largest single war bride organization in the United States is now the Transatlantic Brides and Parents Association (TBPA), started in 1947 in Great Britain by the parents of British war brides. Named the GI Brides', Parents and Friends Association at first, the purpose of this organization was to keep parents and their daughters who had immigrated in touch with each other. Another aspect of the TBPA was applying for discount travel to the United States to visit war brides. In 1966 the United States half of the association formed its own independent division. The club's publicity states that its "purpose is to provide fellowship to our members and to assist them in any way. TBPA also supports charities on local and national levels. Our aims are to foster Anglo-American relationships and continue TBPA as a permanent link with our British heritage."[56] The Transatlantic Brides and Parents Association membership today is predominantly within the United States and Canada, since many of the parents of the war brides have died. The TBPA includes area chapters as well as postal members (women who do not live close to an established branch). One of the more recent projects of the club has been sponsoring war bride reunions in Britain, in 1986, 1989, 1993, and 1995. The association also publishes a monthly newsletter, titled *Together Again,* which keeps the membership informed of the activities of local branches throughout the United States.

War bride clubs have taken many forms, from local to international. Local clubs served the function of counteracting geographic isolation. Since war brides did not settle into British enclaves, they used club affiliation to foster national identity. Most grass roots organizations have found it difficult to continue since new membership has ceased. The TBPA, however, actively recruits new members who are not war brides but daughters of war brides or recent British immigrants. For many women these organizations provided a means of easing their adjustment to life in the United States. Not all British war brides felt the need for, or had the opportunity of enjoying, the company of other women in similar circumstances. Over 60 percent of war brides in the 1989 survey had belonged to war bride clubs at one time and in just over half of these cases the clubs were local.[57]

The nearly 40 percent of British war brides who indicated that they did not join any clubs included women who did not seek association with other war brides. As one upper-class woman noted, "I never considered myself a GI bride. To me it was all those wretched women I travelled with. Many of them were dirty, uneducated and terribly common—though I suppose one doesn't say that these days. You couldn't make chums with them. They were low types who had latched on to the Americans as a way of bettering themselves. Some did."[58] While women of her economic class were rare in the British war bride story, other British women recalled that they wanted to avoid the bride clubs for other reasons. For some women the clubs seemed filled with women who "fed on each other's homesickness."[59] Some British women were too busy to join, noting their need to stay home and take care of the children and household. One woman recalled that she did attend a war bride club meeting in the 1950s but did not join because "the women all seemed to be 'from the North' and . . . this, to a Londoner, was about as different as the company I was in here in the United States."[60]

Not joining clubs could reflect anything from a woman's ease in adjusting to life in the United States to the unavailability of nearby organizations. Rosa Ebsary avoided the clubs on the advice of her

German-American mother-in-law, who grew up in Minnesota. The mother-in-law had seen immigrant communities at first hand. She admitted to her daughter-in-law, "I can't tell you what to do, but as a child I saw a whole generation held back because they didn't mingle, they didn't become Americanized." While war bride clubs did not necessarily represent a threat to Americanization, the war bride in question took the advice but also admitted, "I had had it with war brides by the time I got here. They were a very mixed bag."[61] While not all women joined clubs, over 80 percent of the war brides in the 1989 survey indicated that they had met other British war brides.

It is difficult to conclude whether British war brides were unusual immigrants when it comes to forming clubs and organizations. Many immigration historians mention the importance of clubs to newly arrived immigrants, but a lack of statistics makes it hard to draw conclusions about female immigrant participation rates. As many historians have argued, immigrant clubs can ease assimilation but they can also delay it, by keeping members separate from the wider community. Club members could act as substitutes for the family networks that war brides left behind, however. For most war brides their clubs were a way of overcoming isolation by mixing with other women in similar circumstances. Interestingly, women whose participation in war bride clubs waned usually link this to an increase in family responsibilities. Yet, clubs were only one aspect of the immigrant experience for war brides.

All of these early experiences had an impact on the war brides' transition to life in America. Cultural assimilation, or the outward signs of conforming to the dominant culture, takes place in several stages and is based on a variety of factors. Few immigrants migrate without having an image of the area to which they are moving. Their image may be inaccurate but they have an image nonetheless, and this perception informs their expectations and affects their initial adjustment. The issue is complex for war brides because their expectations involved both marriage and immigration to America. Their expectations of either one or both could have been wrong. A little over half the war brides in the 1989 survey said they knew about the United States before immigrating, based on information they had gained from movies, books, and, to a lesser extent, GI stories. Nearly half the women believed their knowledge was inadequate, perhaps because some of it came from Hollywood and GI stories. Other means they had of learning about the United States included their parents, relatives in the United States, in-laws, school, work, newspapers, and the radio. The orientations that agencies provided and the pamphlets available to war brides were generalized and, therefore, often unhelpful. Hence, many war brides arrived in the United States, like other immigrants before them, without a firm understanding of American society and culture. While conclusions can be drawn about war brides' expectations of America, the question of marriage expectations is less clearcut because the women's ideas of marriage were shaped, as most people's are, individually. Therefore, the issue of marriage adjustment has less to do with immigration and more to do with personalities.

Cultural assimilation in its early stage is also affected by immigrants' early experiences, which, for British war brides, meant their reception in America and their immediate living arrangements. The national attention and overall positive welcome of war brides by Americans obviously provided them with an experience that is unique in immigration history. Bands played, flags waved, and doors opened, but surprises awaited as well. War brides who had arrived in ships full of women in the same circumstances eventually found themselves "alone." The housing shortage forced these women into an intimacy from which there was no escape. If this intimacy included sharing a house or neighborhood with people who did not speak English, the adjustment to life in America could be even more difficult. Unlike other immigrant groups, the war brides did not have the advantage of settling into British enclaves to help ease early adjustment. They went their separate ways instead. While clubs and organizations may have helped with feelings of isolation, the process of conceptual assimilation involves the individual and not the group. Although some of their circumstances differed from those of previous immigrants, the challenge they faced was similar: they needed to learn to understand American society and to find their place within it.

8

Conceptual Assimilation

So what do women like us do, women from different
countries, when our marriages die, when our husbands
die and our children are somewhere else? We've grown
away from our siblings in the old country, . . . our parents are dead. . . . We wind up as a person who is a geographic schizophrenic, constantly torn between two
countries, never settling, wandering like lost souls.

—Helene Lee, *Bittersweet Decision*

Historians and other academics have generated numerous theories
about the assimilation of immigrants, based on a wide range of indicators such as work, family, religion, and politics. However, the investigation of settlement patterns, membership in immigrant organizations, and participation in politics can only suggest trends. Reliance
on these indicators means that the individual immigrant experience
is overlooked. Does the movement of a Swedish immigrant from in-
ner-city Chicago to the suburbs twenty years later indicate assimilation? Does the Irish immigrant's participation in politics denote assimilation? An equally important, but largely underexplored, aspect
of assimilation is the manner in which the immigrants themselves
perceived the process. As Harold Abramson has pointed out, "The
nature of ethnic change for the individual has been relatively overlooked." Vera Audrey Cracknell Long, a war bride and author, has
commented that she had never thought of herself as an immigrant.[1]
Her attitude is understandable since most war brides were immigrating to the United States not as an act of intended migration but as
part of the act of marriage. In this case, immigrants' perceptions of
assimilation are extremely important. One could argue that this conceptual approach is vital in other immigration research as well.

Obviously, the availability of sources would limit historians addressing immigrant perceptions, but researchers into modern immigration

have the opportunity to ask questions of the immigrants themselves. Recent scholarship has recognized the importance of individual immigrants' views and often this research relates to women, since female migrants have dominated American immigration since the 1930s. Oral histories have played a major role in this new scholarship.[2] However, discussions of assimilation often rely on the long-term impact of migration, hence the immigrant group needs to be resident in the United States long enough for the forces of assimilation to have taken hold. British war brides, who have lived in the United States for fifty years, provide an important source of information about both immigrant perceptions and the female immigrant experience.

Any definition of assimilation is fraught with problems. Historians and other scholars are constantly devising and revising terminology for use in the study of immigration. In the present study, assimilation is discussed in two stages, using the terms "cultural assimilation" and "conceptual assimilation." This approach accounts for the existence of stages in assimilation while avoiding the dilution of the process beyond the point of meaningful conclusions. Cultural assimilation, as applied in this case study, denotes outward signs of conforming to the dominant society such as adopting methods of dress, manners, and customs, and even changing to American religious or work patterns. The second stage, conceptual assimilation, suggests that ethnic or national identity has been transformed. The immigrant now identifies more with the receiver rather than the sender country. In this instance the immigrant would no longer see himself or herself as a foreigner or even a hyphenated resident but rather as a full member of the adopted country.

What does this mean for British war brides? Many people have suggested that the processes of assimilation were easier for British immigrants than for other immigrant groups. Moreover, since the war brides were so young when they came to America, the transition should have been smoother. On the other hand, other historians argue that the female immigrant has a harder time adjusting due to the isolation of women within the domestic sphere. In addition, since the war brides did not end up in immigrant enclaves, they did not have the support mechanism or, conversely, the isolation that can accompany an ethnic community.

The stories of the British war brides both compare and contrast with the experiences of other immigrants to the United States. The first stage, or cultural assimilation, has two interrelated aspects. In the case of British war brides, often the first year was very difficult with regard to feelings of loneliness and isolation. However, adjustment to everyday life in the United States, such as dress, manners, and customs, occurred quickly. The second stage, or conceptual assimilation, however, was far harder for the women. British war brides, like immigrants of various other nationalities and eras, confronted significant problems in the last phase of the transition to becoming an American.

As shown earlier, the early days of immigration could be traumatic. It was in the first year or so that the British war brides had the most difficulty with the decision to emigrate. Certainly many women recall that the first step off British soil and onto the ship started a flood of emotion. One woman remembered that "it had been such a tearful goodbye and when the land began to disappear, I panicked. All the things Mum had been trying to tell me about my being so far away and her not being able to help me, this all came back. And I had to fight the feeling that I should jump ship." The woman recalled "thinking as the boat moved away slowly . . . I'm going to an unknown land to live with a man I hardly know."[3] Once the British war bride arrived in the United States the job of adjusting to a new way of life began. Everything was different in America, from the climate (in most regions) to the products on grocers' shelves. The midwestern extremes of hot and cold overwhelmed most British war brides in that region. Mary Swift, who later moved from Minnesota, recalled that "for seven years I lived in fear. Those terrible summer storms! They reminded me of the bombings, the blitz. When the first blizzard came I thought the world was coming to an end. I had never seen snow like that."[4] Similar reactions occurred from Maine to California.

For other war brides initial adjustment included an incredible shock when they discovered the economic and social backgrounds of their ex-GI husbands. As Americans serving in Britain, the men had dressed alike and had all seemed to display relative wealth. Many war brides were unprepared for the diversity of circumstances they eventually met with in the United States. Some women reunited with civilians who were wearing overalls or jeans, men whose families lived in relative poverty. One war bride described her circumstances in America as "living in a shack with a resentful mother-in-law and an alcoholic husband"; another recalled that "home for me was a wooden shack with an outside loo in a tiny mining village. It was difficult to adjust to life there. I was on my own for months."[5] Joan Posthuma commented, "I never went hungry in my life until I came over here."[6] For these women, life in America could mean hardship.

Not all war brides ended up in poverty and many of those who experienced hardship in the early years went on to lead comfortable lives later. Twenty-five percent of the British war brides in the 1989 survey indicated that their standard of living declined when they moved to America. This statistic contradicts the idea that British war brides married rich Americans. Conversely, it does not verify that British war brides did not believe their husbands were rich or at least comfortable in economic terms when they married them.

While a minority of war brides faced a lower standard of living or outright poverty, other problems touched the majority. They all had to adjust to the loneliness and isolation associated with the decision to leave their families and their country behind. A kind reception from the GI's family could offset many difficulties or, on the other hand, in-laws could make the war bride's adjustment harder. Whatever the reception, by family and strangers, the women were for the most part on their own to deal with their emotional turmoil. Helene Lee observed that this problem was faced by all World War II war brides and explained that

> it was the women who gave up parents, sisters, brothers, life-long friends and other relatives, not the husbands. It was the women like Jane, who came from the south of England with its temperate climate, and settled in the plains of Canada to fight snow drifts higher than her house; or Helen, who also came from England and felt as though she would be cooked alive in the heat of New Mexico. Neither did the men give up a life-long religion or substitute the Episcopal Church for the Church of England. The men gave up nothing.
>
> It was the women who gave birth in a strange land, when they would have preferred to be home at that time and have their mothers with them.[7]

British war brides tell stories that document many of these claims. Club membership and kind in-laws could not entirely compensate for the absence of family and friends. For most women the first year in the United States was the most difficult. Not only were the British war brides trying to adapt to life in a foreign country, but they were also beginning married life and having children. Their natural support systems, family and friends, were thousands of miles away. One war bride recalled that on the morning she gave birth to her daughter, "I just lay in the bed and I sobbed for hours."[8] Several women remember the first weeks and months as filled with tears. Very often their husbands did not fully appreciate their situation. Commenting on the isolation, a war bride remembered that "when my husband went to work and I was alone with the baby, everything began to sink in, what

I had done, moved so far away from my home and my parents. I really did not know anyone and I began feeling very lonely, very homesick."[9] Ivy Hammers recalled that the move "was more than I expected and I became, well, ill. Loneliness made me ill. So Ted took me to the doctor and the doctor said, 'Well, your wife is just lonely.' And this was true."[10]

One-third of the war brides in the 1989 survey considered returning to Britain. This high potential return rate signifies the intense trauma of the immigration experience. Mark Wyman suggests that the return rate of earlier English-Welsh immigrants was 19 percent.[11] Statistics on the return migration of British war brides are beyond the scope of this study since the war brides in the survey were women who opted to stay. Yet, one-third considered returning, usually within the first four years of their arrival in the United States.[12] The major reason war brides gave for wanting to go home was an overwhelming homesickness for the familiar surroundings of their native country. Peggy Virden recalled that she "cried and cried, oh, I just didn't like it there. . . . It was a little tiny town and I had come from that great big university town and I just didn't like that at all. I used to beg my husband to send me home but he didn't have any money. I would have to pay my own fare back by that time."[13] War brides who considered returning but did not go back usually indicated lack of money as the determining factor in their decision to remain in America. War brides cited other reasons besides homesickness as motivations for their urge to leave the United States, including incompatibility with their husband, dislike of American culture, the reception they received from in-laws, living conditions, disappointment, or the discovery that their husbands were alcoholics or, in one case, a gambler.

The majority of war brides, on the other hand, had few problems with adjustment (see table 4). A variety of factors could ease the adjustment to life in America. Margaret Wharton credited her relatively easy adjustment to being "older and more mature than most who were wed at 18 or 19. I had had somewhat more education too and several years of experience in a career easily transferable from one country to the next."[14] A welcoming reception also eased the way. Molly Tagart, who arrived on that first bride ship, the SS *Argentina,* remembered a friendly welcome. She claimed her adjustment was eased upon arrival because, "when you walk into a house and a little child that's only five walks up to you, and just looks at you, she's never seen you before in her life, and yet says, 'Hi, Aunt Molly, you're late.' I just started crying. It made me feel so good."[15]

Regardless of the circumstances, the war brides who took part in

Table 4. War Bride Adjustment to the United States

	Easy	Okay	Difficult	Very Difficult
War brides	38%	39%	19%	5%
GIs	56	30	9	3

the survey stayed in America, even those who contemplated returning. However, the question becomes, Did these British immigrants
assimilate? Perhaps the best way to determine the answer to this question is to examine three related issues in relationship to conceptual
assimilation: how the British war brides viewed the adjustment process; whether they would make their decisions if given their lives to
lead over again; and how they see themselves today regarding their
cultural affiliations.

The British war brides in the survey found adjustment to marriage
and motherhood easier than adjustment to life in a foreign country.
Perhaps the women found that adjustment easier because it was a role
they expected to play. When war brides were growing up in the 1930s
their futures in Britain would have presumably included marriage and
children. This was the expectation of most women regarding their
role in society. On the other hand, these British war brides did not
grow up expecting to leave Great Britain. Emigration had not been
part of their future dreams or expectations. Equally significant is the
data that the GIs provided in their survey responses. The difference
in perceptions of ease of adjustment to life in the United States says
much about the loneliness of those involved in the immigration process. Not all women who emigrated because of marriage to a foreigner necessarily had the comfort of a partner who understood their
problems.

Perhaps the women did not convey their distress clearly or perhaps
the men did not comprehend the full impact of loneliness on their
wives. One war bride confessed, "It took me 35 years to get over being homesick. You're busy, your husband is good, your kids are good.
But there's always a pull and I defy anybody to say anything different."[16] Nevertheless, these women remained in the United States.
Their decisions to stay help illustrate the emotions involved in immigration and assimilation. The overwhelming majority of the war
brides revealed that they stayed in the United States because of their
husbands and children.[17] Other, less common reasons for remaining

included starting a career, things getting better, having no place else to go, having no money to return, or reuniting with relatives who had immigrated to the United States.

Indeed, separation from or reunion with family played a major role in the assimilation process. Some women said that they did not have anyone left in Britain to whom they could return. These women were either orphans or only children whose parents were no longer alive. For these few women the pull to return to Britain was minimal. One woman noted that her mother was dead and her father remarried, so, she said, "I was on my own from 14 years old" and coming to America "seemed a great opportunity."[18] For another small minority of British war brides their families followed in their footsteps and emigrated themselves. Some women reported that their parents eventually came to the United States and settled; others mentioned the eventual immigration of sisters and brothers. Still others already had relatives in the United States—aunts and uncles, nieces and nephews. One woman from Northern Ireland recalled that when she first arrived she looked forward to meeting relatives already in the United States and hoped "that very soon my Mother, Brother and Sisters in Ireland will be able to join me here."[19]

The companionship of family members could ease the trauma of immigration but the majority of war brides had left their families behind. This separation from family members, especially a mother and father, caused the most pain by way of loneliness. The separation from parents also entailed an additional burden of guilt. One British war bride noted on her questionnaire form that "the toughest part was being away from our families and as they call it now, 'support system.' The guilt of having our parents grow old and, in my case, the only girl in the family who could help them. This still bothers me even though both of them passed on years ago. This has bothered some of the others also—we have talked about it."[20] Thoughts of the future illness or death of a parent were remote when the war brides were young and made the decision to immigrate. However, as one British war bride confessed, when these inevitable events occurred years later, "it is impossible to describe the intense feelings of guilt, coupled with the overwhelming sense of loss, that develops when it is impossible for whatever reason, to be with one's family at such sad times. When my parents died, none of the valid reasons for my absences helped to alleviate this feeling."[21]

For these women, the immigrant experience did not end with time. Adjustment was a continual process that they faced throughout their lifetimes as important events occurred in both Britain and the United States. That guilt could continue for a long time was evidenced by Molly Tagart, who said that she manages the separation from her elderly mother by keeping "in touch with her doctors and everything, but she's in a house all by herself and she's ninety-one years old. . . . The day when she was so depressed I said to my husband, 'I feel so guilty, feel I should be there.' There are times when I do feel very guilty, I feel that I should be with her. . . . I never really thought she would hang on longer than six months [after my father's death] because my dad was her whole life after I left. But she has hung on a long time."[22]

A potential method of easing feelings of guilt is to make return visits. A large proportion of the British war brides—96 percent—make return trips to their native country. As observed by various immigration researchers, the ability to return to one's country of origin aids in relieving the isolation of immigration. However, the researcher needs to keep several points in mind when discussing the large number of British war brides who make return trips. First, as noted earlier, the ability to make return trips to Britain was not a factor when most of these war brides made the initial decision to immigrate to the United States. For the majority of women, deciding to leave Britain in the mid-1940s meant weighing the desire to reunite with a husband against the prospect of never seeing family again. The age of relatively economical jet travel had not arrived. A return trip to Britain would have required a great deal of time and expense. Most women who left Great Britain did not do so thinking that they would be returning whenever the desire struck them.

Second, the majority of women who returned to Britain for visits did so only after several years' residence in the United States. For most couples the years immediately after the war consisted of lean economic times. Subsequently, with the arrival of children, money was often scarce and trips to Britain were a luxury few could afford. Hence, the majority of British war brides who have returned to visit their homeland did so long after the initial trauma of immigration, when they could better afford these trips, usually by middle age or retirement.

Third, the return to one's native country for visits can affect immigrants in a variety of ways. It can either reinforce the loneliness and homesickness that many immigrants experience or it can emphasize the ways the immigrant has changed and been influenced by the new culture in the adopted country. Doris Weatherford, in *Foreign and Female: Immigrant Women in America,* wrote that "even those who returned because they wanted to often found that home was not as they remembered it. Their experiences abroad had affected them and they no longer 'fit in' at home. . . . A returnee could become a person without a country; no longer happy in the Old World, yet unwilling to accept the New."[23]

This conclusion is as valid for twentieth-century British war brides as for any other immigrant group. By 1970 most British war brides had spent more of their lives in America than they had in Britain. One war bride remembered that when she returned to Britain she "didn't like the English anymore, they were too picky."[24] Yet another war bride said that she "never realized how well I eventually adapted to my life in the States until 1980, when I was last home in England. I just couldn't wait to get back."[25] Yet, other war brides had the opposite experience. Returning to Britain reinforced the sadness of a decision made so many years before. For example, one British war bride recalls that her children "love the land and people I left so easily at age 20. I have not regretted these last 44 years here, but would be the first to pack if Walter said let's go. . . . I feel we girls sacrificed so very much to leave our secure world to live this big adventure."[26] One GI noted that his wife is "just a visitor to the US and to our marriage."[27]

Having considered the adjustment process, one can also evaluate assimilation from the immigrant's perspective by looking back to determine if immigrants would make the same decisions. Since war brides immigrated as an act of marriage, this aspect of adjustment involves two interrelated issues: deciding to marry an American and deciding to immigrate to the United States. In the 1989 survey of British war brides, two questions address this point: Knowing what you know now, would you marry an American, and would you immigrate? The GIs also answered a question on marrying a foreign woman. There is a discrepancy between husbands' and wives' responses on the issue of marriage (see table 5). The difference in perceptions is explainable since it was the women who had made the sacrifice of immigration. Yet, 87 percent of British war brides do not regret marrying an American GI.

The war bride responses to the related question about deciding to immigrate to the United States help to highlight the impact of immigration. Fewer women would immigrate if they had their lives to live over. One British war bride commented that she would agree to marry her husband again, but she also said that she "would have wanted my GI to stay in Great Britain and make a life there, because of homesickness."[28] Another war bride faced with the question of living her life again noted the reasons for the gulf between a war bride response and a GI response about marrying again. She wrote:

Table 5. Reconsidering Decisions

	Yes	No
War brides: Looking back, would you have made the same decision to marry an American GI?	87%[a]	11%[a]
GIs: Looking back, would you have made the same decision to marry a British woman?	96	4
War brides: Looking back, would you have made the same decision to emigrate to the United States?	80	20

a. Two percent of the war brides were unsure whether they would marry a GI again.

Would I do it again? My husband does not understand why I find this such a difficult question to answer. Without any hesitation, he says he would. Actually, why wouldn't he? He never gave up his family or country. He doesn't know what it is to miss them still after all these years, to have missed out on brother's, sister's, and friend's weddings or to be [with] them to share their joys and sorrows, as when my father died. I will always miss England. Admittedly it was my choice to marry him and come here to live. I wonder though, how many of us realized or even thought of what it would be like beyond that immediate thrill of being together with the man you loved in 1946. I know I didn't.[29]

Yet even this woman ultimately decided that she would do it again because "the good parts of my life outweigh the bad." Importantly, the process of immigration, for British war brides, was tied irrevocably to their marital status. To decide not to immigrate would mean to decide not to marry their husbands.

The 20 percent who would not make the same decision to immigrate are adamant about why they feel the way they do. A war bride from New York stated that she believed "Americans don't understand the British and that she would think twice about leaving England" because "it was too great a price to pay."[30] Another bride asserted that she would return to Great Britain when her husband dies. She confesses that she is "still a British citizen and NO, I would never do it again."[31] Indeed, for some female immigrants, the price was too high.

A new life in America did not compensate for leaving family, friends, and the familiarity of a childhood home. Yet the majority of war brides do not feel this way. They look back on that decision in their lives with few regrets.

The question most often asked about war brides is How many marriages ended in divorce? Taking this to refer only to those war brides who immigrated, and not to those who divorced before immigration, the answer is: remarkably few. Of the war brides who participated in the survey, 11 percent divorced their GI husbands. Most of these divorces occurred after 1960, fifteen years after the war was over and fourteen years after most of the war brides came to America. This would seem to indicate that the marriages dissolved due to normal stresses and not because of the incompatibility of national backgrounds or the rigors of immigration. The 11 percent who would not marry a GI again (table 5) are not the same 11 percent who are divorced.[32] It is difficult to draw conclusions from this statistic, however, because the sample may be skewed. There is a possibility that British war brides who returned the questionnaire were those who were satisfied generally with their lives in America. Twenty-seven percent of the women in the survey were widows, which meant they faced life in the United States without the support of the person most responsible for their immigration.

Some historians suggest that citizenship can act as an indicator of immigrant assimilation. Theoretically, immigrants who voluntarily take on a new national identity would have conceptually assimilated; that is, they would now conceive of themselves as American. While the majority of British war brides did become United States citizens, many did so for reasons other than national identity. Some war brides applied for citizenship to participate in the political process. Ivy Hammers stated, "I like to be able to vote. . . . I wouldn't run for political office or anything like that, but I like to put my two cents in."[33] Molly Tagart, who gained her citizenship in 1954, recalled:

> I kept putting it off and putting it off. My oldest son was in school and he came home one day and said "Mommy, you have to go vote." I looked at him and I said, "Sweetheart, I can't." "Why can't you?" Then he got very angry at me because I couldn't vote. I said to Vance, "That's it, I've got to do it." I never thought too much about it. I had a permanent visa. . . . I guess in one respect you want to hold on to your birthright, but when it starts . . . affecting your family life is when you have to make changes. It was very important to my son.[34]

This story highlights a significant point about British war bride immigration. British women were able to hold on to their British citizenship. Hence, becoming an American citizen did not mean denying their national identity. A minority of women, however, refused to take this particular step. War brides who applied for citizenship did so eight years after their arrival, on average; some applied as soon as possible after the three-year waiting period while others waited as long as twenty or thirty years. Reciprocal arrangements between the United States and British governments have made the issue of citizen benefits less restrictive; many war brides old enough to have worked in Britain before or during the war are eligible to collect British pensions today. In a sense, then, war brides who became American citizens did so without jeopardizing their rights as British subjects.

The final question in the conceptual assimilation narrative relates to the immigrants' perception of themselves relative to their native and adopted cultures. The war bride survey asked the women how they perceive of their ethnic identity forty-five years after immigrating (see table 6). One can assume that those women who clearly consider themselves to be American have assimilated most completely. Conversely, those who still see themselves as British have not assimilated. One British war bride stated that "it's been a good life, but home is still Newmarket," while another noted that she is "British and proud of it."[35] The vast majority of women fall between the two extremes and think of themselves as neither wholly American nor completely British. These women epitomize the "hyphenated immigrant," in this case the British-Americans.

Interestingly, ex-GIs gave somewhat different responses to the question of how their wives see themselves. The men believed their wives saw themselves as either more American or more British than the women did, contradicting the women's own sense of assimilation (table 6). The most intriguing aspect of this disparity of perception has to do with women who see themselves as still being British. There is a 10 percent difference between women who classified themselves

Table 6. Perceptions of Ethnic Identity

	American	British	Both
War brides	29%	3%	68%
GI husbands	35	13	52

as British and men who classified their wives as such, which raises some interesting questions concerning one's self-image and the image one projects to others. Slightly over half of the men believed their wives saw themselves as both American and British.

The war brides who saw themselves as British traced these feelings to childhood. Joan Posthuma confessed, "Yes, I still think of myself as British. He doesn't understand that. That's one of the things that we do argue about. I still think of myself as being very British."[36] The women who identify themselves as American report that each trip back to Britain reinforces this perception. Rosa Ebsary used the image of marriage to explain her feelings. She noted that she was "definitely American. I get so homesick to get back. . . . When I took my citizenship, Federal Judge Lindberg said something that always stuck in my mind. He said that taking your citizenship was like getting married, you didn't forget your old loyalties to your family but you had new loyalties to your husband and his family. I think that's very apt, that is a very good way of putting it."[37]

Indeed, it is a "very good way of putting it," since British war brides became immigrants as a result of marriage. However, while the majority of war brides see themselves as both American and British, strong feelings of ethnicity still linger. Eileen Cowan believes that "you could never get rid of your Britishness, never. I can go back to England and just fit right in with the British. . . . I hear myself talking, saying words that I haven't heard for years."[38] June Porter said, "As I get older I find I sit here and I get all the English magazines and I tend to get very nostalgic now and remember walks in the country. I remember England, Gloucester, the Cotswolds and I can come to tears."[39] It is hard to tell how much of that nostalgia is a function of aging and how much is due to feelings of not quite belonging. Perhaps aging and nostalgic memory are more complex processes for immigrants. The message, nonetheless, is clear. Conceptual assimilation, or the end of previous ethnic identity, has not occurred for the majority of British war bride immigrants. For these women, their assimilation to life in the United States never happened.

When seventy thousand British women met American men during World War II they set events in motion that would ultimately lead to the war brides' immigration to the United States. Fifty years after the women sailed from Britain they have become part of the larger story of American immigration history. As individual immigrants from various regions of the British Isles they have led unique lives. As a group, however, their experiences have many commonalities. The majority received a friendly reception from the United States government, their in-laws, and the wider community. Only a few faced problems with their American families over religious differences or ethnic backgrounds. Most stayed married to their GI husbands and would do it all again if they had to live their lives over. More than half joined clubs that included women in similar circumstances, while the vast majority return to Britain for occasional visits with friends and families they left behind. The British war brides, as a group, experienced a relatively smooth transition to American society despite many emotional difficulties in the first year. Cultural assimilation was possible even though, or perhaps because, the majority lived with in-laws for that first crucial period of adjustment.

Yet, the British war brides were alone as immigrants. They settled throughout America, from midwestern farms to coastal cities. As an immigrant group they are locked in a time and a place: 1940s wartime Britain. Hence, this group of immigrants to the United States did not have the luxury of renewing their numbers. There was no established British female immigrant community to join and none to follow. If you ask them who or what they are, the majority tell you they are British-Americans. They conceive of themselves as hyphenated Americans with membership in two societies, as citizens of two countries. Conceptual assimilation has not taken place. They made the decision to marry and to immigrate, but not because they wanted to leave Britain or stop being British.

The one question unasked so far concerns the war bride motivation for immigration. This issue applies to all migrants, regardless of group or era under study. The historian of more recent immigration can ask the participants themselves. As has been argued throughout this study, the perceptions of the immigrants are a valid part of any research on the subject. The British war bride survey allowed women several options of response to the question of why they married an American and moved to the United States (see table 7). They could list more than one reason, such as economic opportunity, pregnancy, and so on. The overwhelming majority responded that the most important reason they married and immigrated was for love. Molly Tagart noted the impact of love as well as the expectations in marriage when she explained that "his home was here. He had at one time said he would stay over there but why should he stay there? It was just me and my mother and dad. Over here he had all of his brothers and sisters and they all had kids and his home was over here. I wouldn't be giving up one-third of what he would. So no, we came here, that's where our life is. I mean, when I married him I knew that I loved him and you do that."[40]

Table 7. Reasons for Marrying an American and Immigrating to
the United States

	Very Important	Somewhat Important	Not Important
Economic opportunity	1%	20%	79%
Glamorous view of United States	3	12	85
Life in Britain would be difficult	3	18	78
I was pregnant	9	—	90
I loved my GI	99	1	—
Other[a]			

a. Fourteen percent of the women filled in the "other" category, listing reasons such as: adventure, desire to emigrate, curiosity, youth, no men in Britain, and they were alone.

No study of British war brides would be complete without some mention of the relationship between GIs and their foreign-born wives. One British war bride, who echoed the sentiments of thousands, was quick to point out that the conclusion about love as a motivation "'hit the nail on the head.' Most of us married for love and were reluctant to leave our families and homeland."[41] Yet another war bride admitted that she "was nineteen years old, it was a great adventure but mostly it was for love for my husband."[42] This sentiment was echoed by almost all British war brides, even those who had the resources to return if things did not work out. One woman said:

> I thought we would come [to the United States] some time but I didn't think we would come to live. It was interesting for us, I was always one for a challenge. I don't think it worried me and I wasn't worried about coming over because I knew very well that if things didn't work out there was money. I could go home. But we have always grown up [believing] that marriage is sacred and you stick together. . . . We just married. I suppose we were in love or we thought we were. But does anybody really know? I often wonder this.[43]

The preponderance of evidence that suggests immigration is a disruptive and difficult experience also suggests that the decision to undergo so much pain has to be an emotional one. Many women indicated that their move from Britain could never have happened without a strong emotional reason. Why else would they go through all that?

As war brides, these women faced an added burden, not felt by male immigrants, related to their gender role. They came to the United States not only as British immigrants but also as wives of American citizens. This subtle difference meant that they came to the United States alone, without the benefit of immigration with other family members. As a result, British war brides had no family support system when it came to meeting life's major challenges. For women this could mean added difficulty in confronting the challenges of marriage, child birth and child rearing, illness and economic hardship. In addition, these British immigrants faced many of the same problems of adjustment as other immigrants. Most historians have ignored the story of British immigration, mistakenly believing that sharing a language and some parts of history and culture with the United States meant that British immigrants assimilated easily into American culture. The fact is that the British may conform quickly at the stage of cultural assimilation because of an external similarity with Americans, but conceptual assimilation does not occur for most British immigrants. The overwhelming majority of British war brides see themselves as hyphenated Americans, "geographic schizophrenics." Cultural similarity might ease initial adjustment but ethnic identity persists, no matter which culture one leaves and no matter where one goes. For the many British war brides who see themselves as only partially assimilated in America the ultimate solution to their dilemma would be "an island somewhere between England and America. It's terrible to be torn between so many loves."[44]

Appendix:
Research Note

When I began researching the topic of British war brides of World War II, I was unaware of how little information existed about the subject. I located primary sources at both the National Archives in Washington, D.C., and the Public Record Office in London, including the records of the Adjutant General's Office, the American Red Cross, the Chief of Chaplains' Office, and the British Foreign Office. Most of the information contained in these files pertained to difficulties and problems that arose between British women and American servicemen, ranging from securing permission to marry to establishing paternity or initiating divorce proceedings. It quickly became apparent that once I had examined the official record I would have to collect first-hand accounts to provide a balanced history.

I distributed questionnaires to British war brides and their GI husbands to compensate for the negative data in the archival sources. The distribution of the questionnaires requires some explanation. In May 1989 the *Seattle Times* ran an article on my research project. The article included the telephone number of the history department at the University of Washington so that any war brides who wished to participate in my project could contact me. In subsequent weeks the local Seattle article went out over the Associated Press wire and appeared in newspapers across the country. Within days the history department received over one hundred phone calls from war brides throughout the country who wanted to share their stories. I talked to each woman on the telephone and then sent a follow-up questionnaire. In the same year the Transatlantic Brides and Parents Association (TBPA) sponsored a war bride reunion in Southampton, England. Although the TBPA organized the reunion, it did not restrict attendance to its membership. I attended the reunion and distributed questionnaires to participants, many of whom also took extra questionnaires back to the United States to hand out to other war brides from their local areas.

I eventually distributed 272 questionnaires in 1989–90, primarily through these two methods of contact. Each questionnaire, coded to allow anonymity, consisted of three pages of questions for the women and two pages for the men. I guaranteed anonymity out of a hope that the men and women would feel freer to answer the questions honestly. Phone calls and letters cited in footnotes are listed by the number I assigned each. Women who phoned or wrote did not have the opportunity to sign waivers, and I felt it was best to protect their identities in case they wished to remain anonymous.

The questionnaires were distributed at random. Three questionnaires went to women who contacted me after an article appeared in the *University Weekly* (a University of Washington publication), with two returned. The story in the *Seattle Times,* and subsequent nationwide publicity, accounted for 124 questionnaires with 66 returned. The Transatlantic Brides and Parents Association membership received 125 questionnaires with only 27 returned. Miscellaneous contacts accounted for 24 questionnaires with 10 returns. Of the total 272 questionnaires distributed, I received completed returns from 105 war brides and 67 husbands. The sample of GI responses is small, unfortunately, due to the age profile of the veterans. However, those men who did fill out and return their questionnaires provided a much-needed counterpart to information on the war bride phenomenon. The sample size is small for both war brides and GIs; however, it does represent a return rate of over 40 percent.

In addition, I conducted in-depth interviews with nine war brides in the Seattle area. My decision to interview war brides within one particular geographic area was based on financial considerations and time constraints. I recognize that the issue of immigration destination is important but I do not believe that confining my oral histories to one particular region diminishes their reliability. Several of the war brides moved to the Seattle area subsequent to their settlement in the United States and their stories provide a counterpoint to those women who arrived and stayed at their original destinations.

The oral histories and questionnaires, as I have presented them in this volume, are not complete records on their own; they are supplemental to the other sources used in my research. The few personal recollections and memoirs of war brides that have appeared in print provide yet more information on the participants' views of events. I did not collect or analyze the data from the questionnaires, interviews, and memoirs using sociological techniques or statistical tools. My purpose has not been to engage in historical quantification or to conduct a sociological study but rather to gather information supplemental to archival material. Readers will note that this volume contains a high incidence of quoted material. The use of oral histories provides the researcher with the opportunity to explain history in the words of the participants. More important, the immigration theory which I propose (conceptual assimilation) is based on the idea of participants' perceptions. Hence, there is often no substitute for the actual words of the men and the women involved in the British war bride story. The women's responses to specific questions on the survey and their own words in the interviews enhance the story; however, they are not the only source for the majority of conclusions reached in this study.

Notes

Chapter 1: Neglected Voices

1. *Immigration and Naturalization Systems of the United States,* Report of the Committee on the Judiciary (S. Res. 137), Report Number 1515 (Washington, D.C.: Government Printing Office, Apr. 1950), 166–67.

2. Staples to Ryan, 27 Sept. 1945, box 985, American Red Cross, Record Group 200, File 618.4 War Brides Britain, National Archives, Washington, D.C. (hereafter abbreviated as NA), 1.

3. Philip E. Ryan to Newman, 28 Sept. 1945, box 985, American Red Cross, Record Group 200, File 618.4 War Brides Britain, NA. The number fifty thousand appears throughout contemporary sources.

4. For a complete discussion of the survey and its distribution see the appendix.

5. *War Brides and Their Shipment to the United States,* Occupation Forces in Europe Series, 1945–46, Office of the Chief Historian, European Command, Frankfurt-am-Main, Germany, 1947, 56 (Table III), and *Annual Report of the Immigration and Naturalization Service,* Department of Justice, Washington, D.C., for fiscal year ending 1950, Table 9A. The army statistics lump together war brides and war husbands; however, the number of men marrying American servicewomen was relatively small. Far-ranging estimates of the numbers of British war brides of World War II appear in secondary sources: 70,000 in Norman Longmate, *The GIs: The Americans in Britain 1942–1945* (New York: Scribner, 1975), 345; 80,000 in Angus Calder, *The People's War: Britain 1939–45* (London: Panther Books, 1971), 360; 100,000 in Elfrieda Berthiaume Shukert and Barbara Smith Scibetta, *War Brides of World War II* (Novato, Calif.: Presidio Press, 1988), 2. Shukert and Scibetta also suggest 1,000,000 war brides in total but they then go on to note that these numbers are "quite possible but unverifiable." Most recently, David Reynolds has suggested a maximum of 45,000 British war brides based on unpublished sources; Reynolds, *Rich Relations: The American Occupation of Britain, 1942–1945* (London: HarperCollins, 1995), 422.

6. See, for example, Pamela Winfield, *Sentimental Journey: The Story of the GI Brides* (London: Constable, 1984); Helene Lee, *Bittersweet Decision* (Lockport, N.Y.: Roselee Publications, 1985); Vera Audrey Cracknell Long, *World War II Pilgrim Brides from Britain: "The Original GI Brides"* (Vienna, Va.: By the

author, 1988); Margaret Wharton, *Recollections of a GI War Bride: A Wiltshire Childhood* (Gloucester: Alan Sutton, 1984); idem., *Marlborough Revisited and the War Remembered: A G.I. Bride Looks Back* (Gloucester: Alan Sutton, 1987). Elfrieda Berthiaume Shukert and Barbara Smith Scibetta, both daughters of war brides, have written a more general account in their book *War Brides of World War II,* cited earlier.

7. Douglas C. Nord, "In Pursuit of 'Invisible' Immigrants: The Case of British Immigration to the United States," in *Contemporary American Immigration: Interpretive Essays (European),* ed. Dennis Laurence Cuddy (Boston: Twayne, 1982), 221.

8. Anthony T. Bouscaren, *International Migrations since 1945* (New York: Praeger, 1963), 70.

9. Thomas J. Archdeacon, *Becoming American: An Ethnic History* (New York: Free Press, 1983), 109.

10. Ibid., 52.

11. Allan Nevins, ed., *America: Through British Eyes* (New York: Oxford University Press, 1948), 402.

12. Charlotte Erickson, *Invisible Immigrants: The Adaptation of English and Scottish Immigrants in Nineteenth-Century America* (Coral Gables, Fla.: University of Miami Press, 1972), 3.

13. Doris Weatherford, *Foreign and Female: Immigrant Women in America 1840–1930* (New York: Schocken, 1986), 179.

14. Marion T. Bennett, *American Immigration Policies: A History* (Washington, D.C.: Public Affairs Press, 1963), 57.

15. Maxine Schwartz Seller, ed., *Immigrant Women* (Philadelphia: Temple University Press, 1981), 118–19.

16. Weatherford, *Foreign and Female,* 196–97.

17. Seller, *Immigrant Women,* 119.

18. Weatherford, *Foreign and Female,* 2.

19. Ibid., 239.

20. Rita James Simon and Caroline B. Brettell, eds. *International Migration: The Female Experience* (Totowa, N.J.: Rowman and Allanheld, 1986), 14.

21. Seller, *Immigrant Women,* 157–59.

22. Ibid., 16.

Chapter 2: The Second World War in Britain

1. The impact of war on women has been discussed in several works, including Arthur Marwick, *War and Social Change in the Twentieth Century: A Comparative Study of Britain, France, Germany, Russia, and the United States* (New York: St. Martin's, 1974); Penny Summerfield, *Women Workers in the Second World War: Production and Patriarchy in Conflict* (London: Croom Helm, 1984); and Margaret Randolph Higonnet, Jane Jenson, Sonya Michel, and Margaret Collins Weitz, eds., *Behind the Lines: Gender and the Two World Wars* (New Haven: Yale University Press, 1987).

2. Gail Braybon and Penny Summerfield, *Out of the Cage: Women's Experiences in Two World Wars* (New York: Pandora, 1987), 138.

3. Ibid., 146.

4. Summerfield, *Women Workers,* 62.

5. Ibid., 34. Raynes Minns, *Bombers and Mash: The Domestic Front, 1939–1945* (London: Virago, 1980), 31, reports the ages of sixteen to forty-nine.

6. Minns, *Bombers,* 31.

7. Braybon, *Out of the Cage,* 159, and Summerfield, *Women Workers,* 35–36. The government lowered the age limit for the National Service #2 Act to nineteen in 1943, raised it to fifty in 1944, and began to include married women in 1944.

8. Cynthia Enloe, *Does Khaki Become You? The Militarization of Women's Lives* (Boston: South End, 1983), 182, and Summerfield, *Women Workers,* 45, 48.

9. Summerfield, *Women Workers,* 20, 51.

10. Ibid., 130.

11. Ibid., 158; Enloe, *Khaki,* 190.

12. Interview with Eileen Cowan, 20 May 1991, Gig Harbor, Washington.

13. Summerfield, *Women Workers,* 55; Shelley Saywell, *Women in War* (New York: Viking Penguin, 1985), 13. Women workers and members of the armed services in the United States faced the same problem during World War II.

14. Braybon, *Out of the Cage,* 165.

15. *News Chronicle,* 28 Mar. 1940, File TC: Women, I/E, Mass Observation Archives, Sussex.

16. *ATS Report—Attitude of Men,* 29 Jan. 1941, File TC: Women, I/F, Mass Observation Archives, Sussex, 5.

17. Interview with Sybil Afdem, 21 Dec. 1981, Everett, Washington.

18. Reynolds, *Rich Relations,* 99, 174.

19. Lee Kennett, *GI: The American Soldier in World War II* (New York: Warner, 1987), 22.

20. Philip Kaplan and Rex Alan Smith, *One Last Look: A Sentimental Journey to the Eighth Air Force Heavy Bomber Bases of World War II in England* (New York: Abbeville, 1983), 35.

21. "Yanks Who Pay Too Much Chided for Boosting Prices," *Stars and Stripes,* 12 Nov. 1943, 4.

22. Interview with Ted Hammers, 16 May 1991, Sequim, Washington.

23. Letter, 10 Jan. 1943, TC: Politics, 3/D, 1, Mass Observation Archives, Sussex.

24. Interview with Joan Posthuma, 9 May 1991, Seattle, Washington.

25. Letter, 20 July 1944, 1–2, TC: Politics, 3/D, Mass Observation Archives, Sussex.

26. Interview with June Porter, 22 Apr. 1991, Edmonds, Washington.

27. *Time,* 6 Dec. 1943, 36, 39. John Ellis, in *The Sharp End of War: The Fighting Man in World War II* (New York: Scribners, 1980), 233, lists most frequent offenses as being AWOL, misuse of vehicles, nonregulation uniform, theft, drunkenness, and looting.

28. Charles F. Kiley, "How to Stay Out of Trouble," *Stars and Stripes*, 2 Apr. 1943, 2.

29. Special Services Division Army Service Forces, *A Short Guide to Great Britain* (Washington, D.C.: War and Navy Departments, 1942), 5, 11, 29.

30. *Anti-Americanism*, 26 Jan. 1947, FR 2454, 1, and *USA*, 27 June 1941, FR 759, both in Mass Observation Archives, Sussex.

31. *American Troops (Indirect)*, Mar. 1943, TC: Politics 3/F, Mass Observation Archives, Sussex.

32. Ellis, *Sharp End*, 372. Reynolds, in *Rich Relations* (152), suggests GI pay was one-third that of the British Tommy.

33. Interview with June Porter, 22 Apr. 1991, Edmonds, Washington.

34. Margaret Mead, *The American Troops and the British Community: An Examination of the Relationship between the American Troops and the British* (London: Hutcheson, 1944), 10. See also Margaret Mead, "The Yank in Britain," *Current Affairs* 64 (11 Mar. 1944): 4–16.

35. Wharton, *Recollections*, 133.

36. Interview with Sybil Afdem, 21 Dec. 1981, Everett, Washington.

37. "From Crap-Shooting to Rural Harvest, This is the A.E.F. Scene," *Yank*, 9 Sept. 1942, 9.

38. Interview with Rosa Ebsary, 29 Apr. 1991, Seattle, Washington.

39. Interview with June Porter, 22 Apr. 1991, Edmonds, Washington.

40. Reynolds, *Rich Relations*, 276.

41. Minns, *Bombers*, 17.

42. Saywell, *Women in War*, 15.

43. *The Registrar General's Statistical Review of England and Wales for the Six Years 1940–1945*, text, vol. 1, Medical (London: His Majesty's Stationery Office, 1949), 17.

44. Higonnet, et al., *Behind the Lines*, 37, claims the war was eroticized, while Paul Fussell, in *Wartime: Understanding and Behavior in the Second World War* (New York: Oxford University Press, 1989), 109, calls the Second World War heteroerotic, unlike World War I, which he labels homoerotic.

45. Higonnet, et al., *Behind the Lines*, 254.

46. John Costello, *Love, Sex and War: Changing Values, 1939–45* (London: Collins, 1985), 89. Costello states that 15 percent of GIs became repeatedly infected, 15 percent never got infected, and 70 percent "expose themselves only under special circumstances." For women the numbers suggest that 40 percent were celibate, 5 percent were regularly sexually active, and 55 percent had sexual relations occasionally. Costello uses very different language when discussing males and females. In the second survey he notes that 25 percent of men "regularly engaged in sexual intercourse" and 5 percent of unmarried women were "promiscuous."

47. Ibid., 131, 147. Costello suggests 75 percent. See also Richard Malkin, *Marriage, Morals and War* (New York: Arden, 1943), 205. Malkin puts the figure at 70 percent.

48. Minns, *Bombers*, 179.

49. Ibid., 240.

50. Ibid., 242, 243.

51. Ibid., 183, and Costello, *Love, Sex and War*, 203.

52. *Registrar General's Statistical Review of England and Wales for the Six Years 1940–1945*, text, vol. 2, Civil, 79.

53. Costello, *Love, Sex and War*, 214, and Minns, *Bombers*, 199. The Registrar General reported that husbands filed at a rate 34.8 percent higher than that for women.

54. Braybon and Summerfield, *Out of the Cage*, 267, and Minns, *Bombers*, 267. There was a similar increase in marriages in the United States associated with the mobilization of men for the armed services.

55. Interview with Joyce Osnes, 9 Nov. 1980, Everett, Washington.

56. Wharton, *Marlborough Revisited*, 101–2.

57. Costello, *Love, Sex and War*, 75.

58. *American Troops (Indirect)*, Mass Observation Archives.

59. Figures for men in service taken from Braybon and Summerfield, *Out of the Cage*, 210; Angus Calder suggests 50 percent of the British men between the ages of twenty and twenty-five were in the service in 1940, in *The People's War*, 138.

Chapter 3: Overseas Marriages

1. Lt. Col. Albert B. Kellogg, *Marriages of Soldiers [of World War I]*, Army War College, Historical Section, July 1942, box 262, Chief of Chaplains, Record Group 247, File 291.1, Marriages, NA, 1.

2. Ibid., 4–5.

3. George Kent, "Brides from Overseas," *Reader's Digest*, Sept. 1945, 97, suggests eight thousand overseas marriages in World War I.

4. War Department Circular 14, 1 Feb. 1940, box 197, Chief of Chaplains, Record Group 247, File 291.1, vol. 1, Oct. 1920–Jan. 1942, Marriages, NA.

5. Director of Intelligence of the Army Service Forces to Office of the Chief of Chaplains, "Reports on Conditions Overseas to Chief of Chaplains," 3 Mar. 1944, box 195, Chief of Chaplains, Record Group 247, File 250.1, Morals and Conduct (Misc.), vol. 2, Jan. 1944–Dec. 1945, NA.

6. C. E. Brand to Chaplain O'Connor, 29 May 1942, box 197, Chief of Chaplains, Record Group 247, File 291.1, Marriages, vol. 2, 24 Feb. 1942–31 Aug. 1942, NA. The residency requirement before citizenship application was shorter for wives of American citizens than for regular immigrants; most immigrants had to wait five years before applying for citizenship.

7. Jenel Virden, "British War Brides of World War II: A Passing Fad with Post-War Complications" (Master's thesis, Washington State University, 1983), 17–20.

8. Letter to William Arnold, 24 May 1942, box 197, Chief of Chaplains, Record Group 247, File 291.1, Marriages, vol. 2, 24 Feb. 1942–31 Aug. 1943, NA.

9. Ibid.

10. Letter, 28 May 1942, box 197, Chief of Chaplains, Record Group 247, File 291.1, Marriages, vol. 2, 24 Feb. 1942–31 Aug. 1943, NA.

11. Charles Dever, letter in response to questionnaire, attached to memo, Joseph O. Ensrud to Director, Public Relations, War Department, 7 Jan. 1943, "Request for Clearance," box 197, Chief of Chaplains, Record Group 247, File 291.1, Marriages, vol. 2, 24 Feb. 1942–31 Aug. 1943, NA. Presumably this related to marriages in the United States since Dever signed his letter from Fort Monmouth, New Jersey.

12. Chaplain Karl L. Darkey to Chaplain George Rixey, 1 Sept. 1943, box 198, Chief of Chaplains, Record Group 247, File 291.1, Marriages, vol. 3, 1 Sept. 1943–31 May 1944, NA, 1.

13. Frederick W. Hagan to Chaplain Darkey, 14 Sept. 1943, Chief of Chaplains, Record Group 247, File 291.1, Marriages, vol. 3, 1 Sept. 1943–31 May 1944, NA, 2.

14. William R. Arnold to Director of Military Personnel Division ASF, 17 Feb. 1945, "Marriages of Enlisted Personnel," box 198, Chief of Chaplains, Record Group 247, File 291.1, Marriages, NA, 1–2.

15. Charles K. Gamble to Richard F. Allen, 12 Nov. 1943, box 985, American Red Cross, Record Group 200, File 618.4, War Brides Australia, NA, 2.

16. Nyles I. Christensen to Colonel H. H. Baird, 29 Feb. 1944, box 985, American Red Cross, Record Group 200, File 618.4, War Brides Australia, NA, 2–3.

17. Interview with Joan Posthuma, 9 May 1991, Seattle, Washington.

18. Interview with Ivy Hammers, 16 May 1991, Sequim, Washington.

19. J. E. Hengham Park to Foreign Office, 5 Sept. 1944, Foreign Office, 371/42310, Public Record Office, Kew, United Kingdom (hereafter abbreviated as PRO).

20. Some women in my survey were unaware of these aspects of dual citizenship while others were well informed. The retention of British citizenship may perhaps have facilitated the transition to American life by providing the war brides some comfort, knowing they retained certain rights as British subjects.

21. Hengham Park to Foreign Office, 1.

22. *Yank,* 1 July 1942, 2.

23. *Stars and Stripes,* 25 Jan. 1945, iv. Other articles noted in text are contained in *Stars and Stripes,* 3 Oct. 1942, 4, and *Yank:* 7 Jan. 1944, 9; 2 Feb. 1945, 16; 23 Feb. 1945, 18; 2 Mar. 1945, 16; 15 June 1945, 14; 10 Aug. 1945, 14; 21 Apr. 1944, 16; 10 Aug. 1945, 14.

24. R. P. Hartle to Lt. Gen. Andrews, "Reference to letter from Andrews on 13 Apr.," 20 Apr. 1943, Adjutant General's Files, Record Group 332, ETO G-1 Section, NA.

25. Pfc. William F. Sprague, *The Problems of Marriages in the European Theater of Operation,* Apr. 1944, Admin. File 518, Adjutant General's Files, Record Group 332, NA, 12.

26. Interview with Ted Hammers, 16 May 1991, Sequim, Washington.

27. Interview with Rosa Ebsary, 29 Apr. 1991, Seattle, Washington.

28. Interview with June Porter, 22 Apr. 1991, Edmonds, Washington.

29. Interview with Sybil Afdem, 21 Dec. 1981, Everett, Washington.

30. Interview with Rosa Ebsary, 29 Apr. 1991, Seattle, Washington.

31. Interview with Sybil Afdem, 21 Dec. 1981, Everett, Washington.

32. *Yank,* 21 Sept. 1945, 18.

Chapter 4: Gaining Entry to America

1. *Immigration and Naturalization Systems of the United States,* 166–67.

2. Howard K. Travers to Lewis R. Barrett, Mar. 1945, box 984, American Red Cross, Record Group 200, File 618.4, NA, 3.

3. Bell to Margaret Shotton, 29 July 1943, "War Brides," 2, and Edna Mattox, 2 Dec. 1943, "Meeting Regarding War Brides," 2, 4, box 984, American Red Cross, Record Group 200, File 618.4, NA.

4. Robert E. Bondy to Area Administration, 21 Dec. 1943, "War Brides," box 984, American Red Cross, Record Group 200, File 618.4, NA, 2.

5. American Red Cross guidelines on overseas marriages (no title), 29 Jan. 1945, box 984, American Red Cross, Record Group 200, File 618.4, War Brides Australia, NA, 5–10. The British government abolished the exit permit in late September 1945, before the war bride transportation operation began. P. M. Broadmead to Jebs, 26 Sept. 1945, Foreign Office, 371/44657, PRO.

6. American Consulate, Auckland, New Zealand, n.d., "Information: Petition Form 633," box 985, American Red Cross, Record Group 200, File 618.4, War Brides New Zealand, NA.

7. Interview with Ivy Hammers, 16 May 1991, Sequim, Washington.

8. American Red Cross guidelines, 29 Jan. 1945, 13, 15–16. Australia's immigrant quota to the United States was one hundred persons per year.

9. Ibid., 17; Marie Youngberg, 9 Aug. 1944, "Notes on Meeting, August 9, 1944," box 985, American Red Cross, Record Group 200, File 618.4, War Brides Australia, NA, 1–3.

10. Edith Spray, 18 July 1945, "Administration and Supplemental Handbook Information Letter No. 220," box 984, American Red Cross, Record Group 200, File 618.4, NA, 7.

11. Mr. Dickstein, HR 4857 Report No. 1320, 29 Nov. 1945, box 103, Committee on Immigration and Naturalization, Record Group 233, Folder HR4179–HR4857, NA, 1.

12. Ibid.

13. Mr. Mason, 30 Nov. 1945, "Expediting the Admission to the United States of Alien Spouses and Alien Minor Children of Citizen Members of the United States Armed Forces," box 103, Committee on Immigration and Naturalization, Record Group 233, bill files HR79A-D15, Folder HR4179–HR4857, NA, 2.

14. David Reimers, *Still the Golden Door: The Third World Comes to America,* 2d ed. (New York: Columbia University Press, 1992), 21.

15. War Department, 16 July 1946, "Bulletin No. 18," Records of the Adjutant General's Office, Record Group 407, NA, 1.

16. Ibid.

17. Colonel Thompson to DeWitt Smith, 8 Aug. 1946, "Alien Fiancées of United States Servicemen and Veterans," box 984, American Red Cross, Record Group 200, File 618.4, War Bride Operation 1946, NA, 1–2, and American Consulate General Naples, n.d., box 985, American Red Cross, Record Group 200, File 618.4 War Bride Operation MTO 1946, NA, 2.

18. *Stars and Stripes,* 4 Sept. 1944, 3; 11 Sept. 1944, 4.

19. "Australian Brides," *Yank,* 18 Aug. 1944, 14.

20. "GI Wives," *Stars and Stripes,* 8 June 1945, 2.

21. "To Disgusted GI Wife" (separate letter), *Stars and Stripes,* 2 July 1945, 2.

22. "Hubby Protests" and "Now Congressman," *Stars and Stripes,* 3 July 1945, 2.

23. "GI Wives to Go 'Home' Last," *Stars and Stripes,* 18 June 1945, 1.

24. "32,000 English Wives to Sail Atlantic," *Daily Mail,* 30 July 1945.

25. *Stars and Stripes,* 28 Aug. 1945, 4.

26. *Stars and Stripes,* 2 Oct. 1945, 1.

27. "Brides Got GI Ship Space" and "US Officials Sail to Study Task of Transporting Wives," *Stars and Stripes,* 6 Oct. 1945, 4.

28. "'U.S. Doesn't Want Us' Complains the GI Brides," "GI Wives May Be Off Soon," articles from unattributed newspaper in author's possession, Oct. 1945.

29. "GI Brides Stage Rally to Protest 'Run Around,'" *Stars and Stripes,* 12 Oct. 1945, 1, 4.

30. "Want-to-go-home Wives Struggle with Police," *Daily Express,* 12 Oct. 1945.

31. "G.I. Bride States Her Case," *Daily Express,* Oct. 1945.

32. *Daily Express,* 11 Oct. 1945, 2.

33. "They Must Wait Till New Year," *Daily Express,* 13 Oct. 1945.

34. "Send-us-home Wives Get Transport Shock," *Daily Express,* 13 Oct. 1945.

35. Mary Williams to Humphrey Clarke, 11 June 1945, "Recommendation to be Presented to the Commanding General, U.S. Army June 12, 1945," Foreign Office, 371/44657, PRO.

36. W. J. Gallman to P. M. Broadmead, 17 July 1945 and draft reply P. M. Broadmead to W. J. Gallman, 28 July 1945: Foreign Office, 371/44657, PRO.

37. P. M. Broadmead to R. A. Mattson, 15 Aug. 1945, Foreign Office, 371/44657, PRO.

38. Parliamentary Question, 15 Oct. 1945, Foreign Office, 371/44657, PRO.

39. Bennett, *American Immigration Policy,* 87.

Chapter 5: From the Old World to the New

1. *War Brides and Their Shipment,* 34.

2. "Tuesday Fixed as D-Day for an Army of GI Wives," *Daily Mail,* last week of Dec. 1945, and "'Queen' May Carry Home G.I. Brides," ibid., 17 Dec. 1945;

see also "'Joy' Liner Will Take G.I. Brides to U.S.," *Sunday Dispatch,* 16 Dec. 1945.

3. Robert H. Bremner, Minna Adams Hutcheson, and Lucille Stein Greenberg, "American Red Cross Services in the War Against the European Axis, Pearl Harbor to 1947," *The History of the American National Red Cross,* vol. 13 (Washington, D.C.: American Red Cross, 1950), 516–18; Beryl Beringer to Mary B. Moss, 17 Dec. 1945, "GI Brides" box 985, American Red Cross, Record Group 200, File 618.4, War Bride Operation ETO 1946, NA, 1–3.

4. Beringer to Moss, 17 Dec. 1945, cover page.

5. Ibid., 1.

6. "GIs Make Cribs, Nappies, at Brides' Camp," article from unattributed newspaper in author's possession, 1 Jan. 1946.

7. "No Pistol Packing Brides," *Daily Express,* Jan. 1946.

8. "G.I. 'Baby Liners,'" and "G.I. Bride Ship on the Way," articles from unattributed newspaper in author's possession, late Jan. 1946.

9. James L. Bartley to "Dear Madam," no date, box 985, American Red Cross, Record Group 200, File 618.4, War Bride Operations ETO 1946, NA, enclosures, 1; duplicate letter, states, "prepare yourself to travel *at a week or ten days' notice.*"

10. The United States eliminated the need for several vaccinations after an outcry from antivaccination protesters. Parliamentary Question #43, 13 Feb. 1946, 371/51617; and National Anti-Vaccination League, "Vaccinating British Women," 26 Feb. 1946, Foreign Office, 371/44657, PRO.

11. Beringer to Moss, cover page.

12. "344 Brides in Transit Camp," *Daily Telegraph,* 23 Jan. 1946.

13. Interview with Peggy Virden, 8 Nov. 1980, Everett, Washington.

14. Interview with Joan Posthuma, 9 May 1991, Seattle, Washington.

15. Ibid.

16. Interview with Rosa Flisary, 29 Apr. 1991, Seattle, Washington.

17. Ibid.

18. Interview with June Porter, 22 Apr. 1991, Edmonds, Washington.

19. Louise Mumm, 15 Mar. 1946, "War Bride Operation," 1; H. Dorsey Newson, "Minutes of Meeting Held March 15th 1946 New York Port of Embarkation on War Brides," 1, reports the expenses at two to three dollars a day. Both in box 984, American Red Cross, Record Group 200, File 618.4, War Bride Operation ETO 1946, NA.

20. Mumm, "War Bride Operation," 2–3.

21. Julie to "Mum" (copy), 25 Apr. 1946, Foreign Office, 371/51620, PRO, 1.

22. J. Marshall to Parker (copy), 27 Apr. 1946, Foreign Office, 371/51620, PRO, Kew, United Kingdom, 1.

23. "L.A. Vet Blames British Camp in Deaths of Ship Babies," *Los Angeles Herald,* 27 May 1946.

24. Letter to British Consulate-General (copy), 28 May 1946, Foreign Office, 371/51620, PRO.

25. British Consulate General, Los Angeles, to British Embassy, 31 May

1946; British Embassy to North American Department, 10 June 1946; W. J. Ford to B. E. F. Gage, 22 July 1946, Foreign Office, 371/51621, PRO.

26. *War Brides and Their Shipment*, 46.

27. Chester Wordlow, "The Transportation Corps: Movements, Training, and Supply," *United States Army in World War II* (Washington, D.C.: Department of the Army, 1956), 235.

28. Harry Boyte to Ruth Hill, "Staffing Ships for War Brides Transportation," 28 Dec. 1945, box 984, American Red Cross, Record Group 200, File 618.4, War Bride Operation 1943–45, NA, 1.

29. Ruth Hill to C. A. Maupin, "Staffing Recreation Programs on Ships Bringing War Brides," 28 Dec. 1945, box 984, American Red Cross, Record Group 200, File 618.4, War Bride Operation 1943–45, NA, 1. Red Cross personnel originally believed they would be in charge of recreational activities on board the ships but the army representatives on board took over these duties with some shared responsibility with Red Cross staff. Each ship had different shared duties.

30. Vivien S. Harris to Thomas Dinsmore, 12 Jan. 1946, "War Bride Operation," box 984, American Red Cross, Record Group 200, File 618.4, War Bride Operation ETO 1946, NA, 1.

31. "Narrative Report U.S. [*sic*] Argentina," 15 Jan.–4 Feb. 1946, box 985, American Red Cross, Record Group 200, File 618.4/08, War Bride Ship Reports, NA, 2.

32. Vivien S. Harris to John Potts, n.d., "War Bride Operation SS Argentina, SS Queen Mary," box 984, American Red Cross, Record Group 200, NA, 3.

33. "Narrative Report U.S. [*sic*] Argentina," 2.

34. Interview with Peggy Virden, 8 Nov. 1980, Everett, Washington.

35. Interview with Rosa Ebsary, 29 Apr. 1991, Seattle, Washington.

36. "Bride's Diary Tells of Voyage," *New York Sun*, Feb. 1946.

37. Interview with Eileen Cowan, 20 May 1991, Gig Harbor, Washington.

38. Article from unattributed newspaper in author's possession, 27 Jan. 1946.

39. Interview with June Porter, 22 Apr. 1991, Edmonds, Washington.

40. "Narrative Report U.S.A.T. E. B. Alexander," 11 Apr.–1 May 1946, box 985, American Red Cross, Record Group 200, File 618.4/08, War Bride Ship Reports, NA, 2–3. Attempts to resolve problems and the extent of some of these problems are discussed in greater detail in chapter 6.

41. "Bride's Diary Tells of Voyage," *New York Sun*, Feb. 1946.

42. Mildred Von Wynen to Louise Mumm, 21 Feb. 1946, box 984, American Red Cross, Record Group 200, File 618.4, 1946, NA, 2.

43. Ibid.

44. Ibid., 3.

45. Eugene O. Fosdick to Wm. S. Hepner, 22 Apr. 1946, "War Brides," box 984, American Red Cross, Record Group 200, File 618.4, 1946, NA.

46. Harris to Potts, "War Bride Operation SS Argentina," 2. As with each subsequent trip, the American Red Cross staff on board filed a short narra-

tive report on the crossing that detailed the functions Red Cross personnel performed for the war brides and children and any special problems that arose during the voyage. The estimates of the number of brides and children on board the SS *Argentina* vary with different accounts and sources. I have relied here on the "official count" provided by the American Red Cross Assistant Director for Home Service at Red Cross National Headquarters who was on board the ship.

47. *New York World Telegram,* 4 Feb. 1946, 12; *New York Journal America,* 4 Feb. 1946; *New York Times,* 5 Feb. 1946, 25.

48. Article from unattributed newspaper in author's possession.

49. "458 British War Brides and 175 Babies Arrive to Set Up New Homes in U.S.," *New York Sun,* 4 Feb. 1946, 1, and "Fathers and Stuffed Animals Kept Waiting," *New York Sun,* 4 Feb. 1946.

50. "Anxious Husbands Arrive Early for Reunion with War Brides at the Red Cross House Here," *New York Times,* 5 Feb. 1946, 25.

51. Ibid., and Harris to Potts, "War Bride Operations SS Argentina," 4.

52. DeWitt Smith to various Red Cross personnel, 12 Apr. 1946, "War Bride Operation," box 984, American Red Cross, Record Group 200, File 618.4, 1946, NA, 3.

53. Rose N. Dunn to David Conklin, 7 Feb. 1946, "Train War Brides," box 984, American Red Cross, Record Group 200, File 618.4, 1946, NA, 2.

54. Various documents within American Red Cross, Record Group 200, box 984, File 618.4, 1946, NA: Margaret Alback to D. Atchison Keeler, 7 Feb. 1946, "Train Service"; Agnes Lindsay to David O. Conklin, 7 Feb. 1946; Margaret H. Daniels to Mr. D. Acheson Keeler, 28 Feb. 1946, "Train Service"; Mary I. Ward to Miss Council, 13 Feb. 1946.

55. Interview with Joan Posthuma, 9 May 1991, Seattle, Washington.

56. Chart, 2 Apr. 1946, box 985, American Red Cross, Record Group 200, File 618.4, War Bride Operation, NA.

57. Interview with Margaret Ripper, 22 Dec. 1991, Everett, Washington.

58. Interview with Joan Posthuma, 9 May 1991, Seattle, Washington.

59. R. O. Purves to F. A. Winfrey, 10 Oct. 1945, "Dependents and Fiancées of Servicemen and Veterans Coming to the United States (War Brides)," box 984, American Red Cross, Record Group 200, File 618.4, War Bride Operation 1943–45, NA, 6–7.

60. Captain William J. Lee to Don C. Smith, 5 Mar. 1946, "War Brides-Communications Concerning," box 984, American Red Cross, Record Group 200, File 618.4, 1946, NA, 2.

61. Kay Schueller to Charlotte Johnson, 30 Oct. 1946, "Discontinuance of Army Transportation of War Brides from the United Kingdom," box 985, American Red Cross, Record Group 200, File 618.4, War Bride Operation ETO 1946, NA, 1.

62. Wilbur S. Elliott to General Stockston, 12 Nov. 1946, box 985, American Red Cross, Record Group 200, File 618.4, War Bride Operation ETO 1946, NA.

Chapter 6: Transatlantic Divorce, Paternity, and Incomplete Immigration

1. "Girls Left by U.S. Husbands," 6 Dec. 1943, unidentified newspaper, box 985, American Red Cross, Record Group 200, File 618.4, Australia, NA.

2. William R. Arnold to Commanding General ETOUSA, 18 Apr. 1944, "Investigation," Chief of Chaplains, Record Group 247, File 291.1, Marriages, NA.

3. European Theater of Operation United States Army, 15 Mar. 1944, Circular 57, Foreign Office, 371/42310, PRO.

4. R. A. McWilliams to Marshall Son and Bulgin, 23 Sept. 1944, Foreign Office, 371/42310, PRO.

5. R. N. Greathead, Jr. to Colonel Kenneth Mackessack, 3 Aug. 1945, Foreign Office, 371/51618, PRO, 1.

6. "Separation," *Yank*, 7 Sept. 1945, 21.

7. M. E. Bathurst, 6 Mar. 1946, "Memorandum on G.I. Brides," Foreign Office, 371/51618, PRO, 1.

8. Ibid., 34.

9. "Matrimonial Causes (War Marriages) Act, 1944 and Existing Provisions for Legal Aid in Divorce and Matrimonial Causes" (copy), n.d., Foreign Office, 371/511619, PRO, 1.

10. W. H. G., 23 Mar. 1946, "G.I. Brides," Foreign Office, 371/511619, PRO, 2–3.

11. "G.I. Brides and Unmarried Mothers. Legal and Financial Aid," late 1946, Foreign Office, 371/51622, PRO, 2.

12. Catherine Schueller, 29 July 1947, "Conference Held July 21 re: War Brides," box 985, American Red Cross, Record Group 200, File 618.4, Australia, NA, 1.

13. Quoted in Mary M. Rogers to Charlotte Johnson, 8 Feb. 1946, "Addresses of Men in Service," box 984, American Red Cross, Record Group 200, File 618.31, NA, 1–2.

14. Major Bramall, 11 Oct. 1946, Parliamentary Question 10, Foreign Office, 371/51622, PRO.

15. Appendix A, "Notes on State Laws Regarding Affiliation Proceedings," n.d., Foreign Office, 371/61016; Foreign Office to British Embassy Washington, D.C., 3 Feb. 1947, "#1046," Foreign Office, 371/61017, PRO, 1.

16. Chancery to North American Department, 12 Feb. 1947, Foreign Office, 371/61017, PRO.

17. Chancery to North American Department, 4 Dec. 1947, Foreign Office, 371/61021, PRO, 1.

18. B. E. Astbury, n.d. (early 1947), "Statement Circulated by Family Welfare Association of Great Britain to Cooperating Family Agencies," box 984, American Red Cross, Record Group 200, File 618.31, NA.

19. J. Charrow, 9 Apr. 1947, "Apportionment of Benefits under GI Bill of Rights to Illegitimate Children of Veterans," box 984, American Red Cross, Record Group 200, File 618.31, NA.

20. Chancery to Consulates, 12 May 1947, Circular No. 47, Foreign Office, 317/61019, PRO, document and attachment.

21. E. Gwynn to "Dear Sir or Madam," 16 Feb. 1948, Foreign Office, 371/68045A, PRO, 1.

22. Chancery to North American Department, 18 May 1948, Foreign Office, 371/68045A, PRO, 1.

23. Foreign Office to U.S. Embassy, 23 Feb. 1946, "GI Brides, Note by the Home Office," Foreign Office, 371/61617, PRO, 1.

24. Miss Arnold to Field Consultants, 24 Oct. 1945, "Children of United States Military Personnel and Veterans Living Outside the United States," box 984, American Red Cross, Record Group 200, File 618.31, NA, 1.

25. Marie Youngberg to Charlotte Johnson, 7 Mar. 1946, "Meeting with U.S. Children's Bureau—March 4, 1946," box 984, American Red Cross, Record Group 200, File 618.31, NA. Italics added.

26. W. M. G., 14 Dec. 1945, "Coloured Children of English Mothers and Negro Members of the United States Forces," Foreign Office, 371/51617, PRO, 1. Of the thirty-seven cases of mulatto orphans in Somerset Residential Nursery, twenty-seven of them were born to married women.

27. Ibid., 2.

28. Many years after the war some of the illegitimate children of American GIs began organized searches for their fathers. In 1984, two different British organizations, War Babes and Transatlantic Children's Enterprise (TRACE), began an attempt to locate American fathers of British children. Some individuals have met with success, but others have encountered problems. Often these adult children have very little information about their fathers beyond name, service unit, and perhaps hometown and state. Requests from British subjects for information about Americans do not meet with much enthusiasm from United States government officials even to today. The American government sees this as a privacy issue, while the "children" see it as a personal, family history quest. The government has granted access to records under the Freedom of Information Act in recent years. See Pamela Winfield, *Bye Bye Baby: The Story of the Children the GIs Left Behind* (London: Bloomsbury Publishing Ltd., 1992).

Another problem for many of the searchers is the age of the GI veterans. The longer the search takes, the less likely it becomes that the men are still alive. Publicity afforded this small segment of the British population fluctuates with the significant historical anniversaries of World War II. January 1992 marked the fiftieth anniversary of the arrival of the first American GIs in Northern Ireland, hence the quest for information by members of War Babes and Trace received renewed interest, although media coverage in Britain was much higher than that in the United States. Similarly, June 1994 and May 1995, the fiftieth anniversaries of the D-Day and VE-Day respectively, witnessed another public airing of these wartime issues.

29. Letter to Head Nurse (copy), 26 Feb. 1946, Foreign Office, 371/51618, PRO.

30. Edna Mattox to Charlotte Johnson, 12 Feb. 1944, "SAF 274, War

Brides," box 984, American Red Cross, Record Group 200, File 618.4, NA, 2.

31. American Red Cross guideline, 29 Jan. 1945, 22.

32. Edith Spray to Home Service Workers and Field Directors, 18 July 1945, "Alien Wives and Fiancees of Servicemen," box 984, American Red Cross, Record Group 200, File 618.4, NA, 20.

33. St. Louis Consulate to British Embassy, 15 May 1946, Foreign Office, 371/51620, PRO.

34. P. H. Gore-Booth to North American Department, 30 July 1945, Foreigh Office, 371/44657, PRO, 2.

35. Ibid., 1.

36. J. N. Knox to F. B. A. Rundall, 17 July 1947, Foreign Office, 371/61021, PRO, 1.

37. North American Department to Chancery, 23 Nov. 1945, Foreign Office, 371/44657, PRO.

38. R. S. B. Best to Edwina Avery, 23 Nov. 1946, Foreign Office, 371/51623, PRO, 3–4.

39. L. M. Nelson to F. B. A. Rundall, 12 Feb. 1947, 1, and Foreign Office to British Embassy, 11 Mar. 1947, "Provisional Instructions to Consular Officers in the United States for the Provision of legal aid to British women married to United States servicemen or ex-servicemen and who are involved in matrimonial proceedings," both in Foreign Office, 371/51623, PRO.

40. Interview with Peggy Virden, 8 Nov. 1980, Everett, Washington. Other accounts of similar incidents on different ships abound. See American Red Cross ship reports and Corinna Honan, "Princess, peeress, and GI bride," *Daily Mail,* 6 Apr. 1984, 21.

41. R. S. B. Best to Edwina Avery, 23 Nov. 1946, Foreign Office, 371/51623, PRO, 3.

42. *Overseas Wives Doings,* English-Speaking Union of the United States, 1 Oct. 1946, Foreign Office, 371/51623, PRO, 4–5.

Chapter 7: Transitions

1. For a full discussion of assimilation terms and applications see chapter 8.

2. Claire Kerlee, "British Wives, Fiancees Cotton to Un-Hollywoodlike Cottons," *Stars and Stripes,* 11 Dec. 1944, 5.

3. Interview with June Porter, 22 Apr. 1991, Edmonds, Washington.

4. Richard Wilbur, "Pricking a Few Balloons: English Wives of Yanks Get Classes in Americana," *Stars and Stripes,* 6 Apr. 1944, 2.

5. Interview with Peggy Virden, 8 Nov. 1980, Everett, Washington.

6. "Mrs. Roosevelt Gives GI Brides 6–point Behavior Code," *Daily Mail,* 25 Jan. 1946.

7. Bremner, et al., "American Red Cross Services," 513.

8. Charlotte Johnson, "The Start of a New Day," *Red Cross Courier,* Mar. 1946, 4.

9. Judy Barden, "Red Cross Girls Aid Brides," *New York Sun,* 6 Feb. 1946.

10. Barbara Klaw, "GI Brides Find Advice Isn't Rationed," *New York Sun,* 4 Feb. 1946.

11. "Brooklyn? Like a Suburb of London, Says Colleen," *Stars and Stripes,* 2 Oct. 1944, 3.

12. Violet Brown, "Liberty Blazes Salute to British War Brides," *Brooklyn Eagle,* 4 Feb. 1946, 1.

13. *A Bride's Guide to the U.S.A.,* British Good Housekeeping Magazine and the United States Office of War Information, n.d., 5.

14. Ibid., 8.

15. Interview with Peggy Virden, 8 Nov. 1980, Everett, Washington.

16. Interview with Sybil Afdem, 21 Dec. 1981, Everett, Washington.

17. Wharton, *Recollections,* 169.

18. Henry M. Jackson to Harry S Truman, 12 Sept. 1946, Jackson Papers, University of Washington Libraries, Seattle, Washington.

19. Matthew J. Connelly to Congressman Jackson, 14 Sept. 1946, Jackson Papers, University of Washington Libraries, Seattle, Washington.

20. Interview with Molly Tagart, 3 May 1991, Seattle, Washington.

21. Pauline Gardescu to Edith Spray, 28 Feb. 1946, "Citizens Government Conference of the Housing Emergency, February 7–8, 1946," box 984, American Red Cross, Record Group 200, File 618.32, NA, 1–2.

22. Of these, 88 percent lived with their in-laws, 7 percent with other relatives, and 5 percent with other people such as boardinghouse occupants. The average length of time spent living with other people was nine months. Five women are not included in this average. They reported living with other people from four years to fourteen years. If one factors them in, the length of time British war brides and their husbands spent living with other people before getting a place of their own goes up to fourteen months.

23. Interview with June Porter, 22 Apr. 1991, Edmonds, Washington.

24. Interview with Joan Posthuma, 9 May 1991, Seattle, Washington.

25. Jonathan Kilbourn, "Overseas Brides," *Yank,* 16 Nov. 1945, 6–7.

26. Telephone conversation number 6.

27. As for the ethnic backgrounds of the war brides, 80 percent were English, 5 percent Scottish, 3 percent Welsh, 3 percent Irish, and 10 percent a combination of two or more groups.

28. Interview with Ivy Hammers, 16 May 1991, Sequim, Washington.

29. "The Housing Situation," *Overseas Wives Doings,* 2.

30. Interview with Joan Posthuma, 9 May 1991, Seattle, Washington.

31. The war brides in the survey were 87 percent Protestant (62 percent Church of England), 9 percent Catholic, and 4 percent Jewish. For the GIs the numbers were 70 percent Protestant (10 percent Episcopal), 22 percent Catholic, and 3 percent Jewish.

32. Interview with Molly Tagart, 3 May 1991, Seattle, Washington.

33. Kilbourn, "Overseas Brides," 6–7.

34. Rita James Simon, *Public Opinion and the Immigrant: Print Media Coverage, 1880–1980* (Lexington, Mass.: Heath, 1985), 34.

35. Interview with Ivy Hammers, 16 May 1991, Sequim, Washington.

36. Interview with June Porter, 22 Apr. 1991, Edmonds, Washington.

37. Interview with Rosa Ebsary, 29 Apr. 1991, Seattle, Washington.

38. Questionnaire 01F0029.

39. A. Victor Lasky, "GIs Talk Way Home Via Voicecast, Ltd.," *Stars and Stripes,* 19 June 1945, 4.

40. Questionnaire 02F0143.

41. Interview with Ivy Hammers, 16 May 1991, Sequim, Washington.

42. Oscar Handlin, quoted in *Immigrants and American History,* ed. Henry Steele Commager (Minneapolis: University of Minnesota Press, 1961), 15.

43. Interview with Sybil Afdem, 21 Dec. 1981, Everett, Washington.

44. "As Seen at National Headquarters," *English-Speaking Bulletin,* Nov. 1946, 3.

45. Ruth Graham, "British Bride Tells of Welcome in U.S.," *Stars and Stripes,* 2 Oct. 1945, 1.

46. Kilbourn, "Overseas Brides," 7.

47. Untitled, undated document describing "a joint statement of the American Red Cross and the English-Speaking Union defining services and responsibilities," Summer 1945, Foreign Office, 371/51622, PRO, 1.

48. *Overseas Wives: A Cordial Welcome Awaits You,* English-Speaking Union, New York, 2.

49. Chancery to North American Department, 14 Oct. 1946, Foreign Office, 371/51622, PRO, 1.

50. *Red Cross Courier,* Aug. 1946, 21.

51. Interview with Ivy Hammers, 16 May 1991, Sequim, Washington.

52. Interview with Joan Posthuma, 9 May 1991, Seattle, Washington.

53. International Wives Organization scrapbook, Everett, Washington; in possession of May Scougal.

54. Interview with Joyce Osnes, 9 Nov. 1980, Everett, Washington.

55. Interview with Sybil Afdem, 21 Dec. 1981, Everett, Washington.

56. Taken from the TBPA information brochure.

57. That 60 percent of the sample joined clubs seems a high figure, but clubs were one form of contact for questionnaire distribution. However, if women in the survey who were contacted through war bride clubs are eliminated, the percentage of British war brides who joined war bride clubs only drops by 7 percent, to 53 percent.

58. Corinna Honan, "Princess, peeress," 22.

59. Telephone conversation number 7.

60. Letter number 26.

61. Interview with Rosa Ebsary, 29 Apr. 1991, Seattle, Washington.

Chapter 8: Conceptual Assimilation

1. Harold Abramson, "Assimilation and Pluralism," in *The Harvard Encyclopedia of American Ethnic Groups,* ed. Stephan Thernstrom (Cambridge,

Mass.: Harvard University Press, 1980), 150; Vera Audrey Cracknell Long, personal communication to author, 23 Sept. 1993.

2. See Donna Gabaccia, ed., *Seeking Common Ground: Multidisciplinary Studies of Immigrant Women in the United States* (Westport, Conn.: Praeger, 1992), and *International Migration Review* 18 (Winter 1984), special issue devoted to female migration.

3. Lee, *Bittersweet Decision,* 126–27.

4. Mary Swift, "Cancer Crusader Shares 39–year Love Story," *Renton Chronicle,* Apr. 1984.

5. "Meeting War Brides Again Years after Those Wedding Bells," article from unattributed newspaper in author's possession, c. 1984, and L. Warner and Anna Treacher, "Love that Turned to Tears," *Daily Mirror,* 17 Aug. 1989, 13.

6. Interview with Joan Posthuma, 9 May 1991, Seattle, Washington.

7. Lee, *Bittersweet Decision,* 349.

8. Anna Treacher, "Mrs GI Joe," *Daily Mirror,* 16 Aug. 1989, 16.

9. Lee, *Bittersweet Decision,* 206.

10. Interview with Ivy Hammers, 16 May 1991, Sequim, Washington.

11. Mark Wyman, *Round-Trip to America: The Immigrants Return to Europe, 1880–1930* (Ithaca: Cornell University Press, 1993), 10.

12. Repeated attempts to locate significant numbers of British war brides who returned to Great Britain have failed.

13. Interview with Peggy Virden, 8 Nov. 1980, Everett, Washington.

14. Wharton, *Marlborough Revisited,* 121.

15. Interview with Molly Tagart, 3 May 1991, Seattle, Washington.

16. "British Brides of GIs Home after 40 Years," *San Luis Obispo Telegram-Tribune,* 27 Sept. 1986.

17. The percentage who remained for these reasons includes: 24 percent because of children, 36 percent because of husband, 20 percent because of husband and children.

18. Questionnaire 02F0100.

19. "This Is Your Red Cross," Paterson, N.J., 6 Mar. 1947, Radio WPAT, script.

20. Questionnaire 02F0084.

21. Lee, *Bittersweet Decision,* 299.

22. Interview with Molly Tagart, 3 May 1991, Seattle, Washington.

23. Weatherford, *Foreign and Female,* 242–43.

24. Telephone call number 9.

25. Lee, *Bittersweet Decision,* 206.

26. Letter number 22.

27. Questionnaire 02M0197.

28. Questionnaire 03F0010.

29. Lee, *Bittersweet Decision,* 249.

30. Edith Lederer, "War Brides Return to Laughter, Tears," *Progress Bulletin,* 27 Sept. 1986, 4.

31. Lee, *Bittersweet Decision,* 251.

32. Shukert and Scibetta, in *War Brides,* 2, put the rate of divorce among war brides of all countries at 14 percent, based on their distribution of a questionnaire to two thousand women.

33. Interview with Ivy Hammers, 16 May 1991, Sequim, Washington.

34. Interview with Molly Tagart, 3 May 1991, Seattle, Washington.

35. Letter number 19 and postcard.

36. Interview with Joan Posthuma, 9 May 1991, Seattle, Washington.

37. Interview with Rosa Ebsary, 29 Apr. 1991, Seattle, Washington.

38. Interview with Eileen Cowan, 20 May 1991, Gig Harbor, Washington.

39. Interview with June Porter, 22 Apr. 1991, Edmonds, Washington.

40. Interview with Molly Tagart, Seattle, Washington.

41. Letter number 21.

42. Questionnaire 03F0002.

43. Interview with Joan Posthuma, 9 May 1991, Seattle, Washington.

44. Lee, *Bittersweet Decision,* 245.

Bibliography

Any study of British war brides requires the utilization of archival records to show the policies and procedures that various agencies established to handle marriage and immigration issues. Other customary historical resources, such as newspapers and magazines, fill many of the gaps left by official agencies. Such sources, as well as primary and secondary publications and personal memoirs, were used in the present study.

Archival Sources

National Archives
 Record Group 200. American Red Cross.
 Record Group 233. Committee on Immigration and Naturalization.
 Record Group 247. Chief of Chaplains.
 Record Group 332. Records of Historical Division.
 Record Group 407. Adjutant General's Office.
Mass Observation Archives (Sussex)
Public Record Office:
 Foreign Office File 371.
University of Washington Libraries:
 Jackson Papers

Newspapers

Many of the newspaper articles in this study were supplied to the author by the war brides themselves. These women collected newspaper accounts about the war bride phenomenon for their own personal scrapbooks and memories. Hence, many of the newspaper accounts appear without benefit of date, page number, and, occasionally, the name of the publication itself. These sources were used even though they are incomplete, because the information contained in these public accounts was germane to the story.

Brooklyn Eagle
Daily Express (London)
Daily Mail (London)

Daily Mirror (London)
Daily Telegraph (London)
Los Angeles Herald
New York Journal American
New York Sun
New York Times
New York World Telegram
News Chronicle (London)
Progress Bulletin
Reader's Digest
Renton (Washington) *Chronicle*
San Luis Obispo Telegram-Tribune
Sunday Dispatch
The Times (London)

Periodicals

International Migration Review
The Red Cross Courier
Stars and Stripes
Time
Yank

Books and Pamphlets

Annual Report of the Immigration and Naturalization Service. Washington, D.C.: Department of Justice, 1950.

Archdeacon, Thomas J. *Becoming American: An Ethnic History.* New York: Free Press, 1983.

Bennett, Marion T. *American Immigration Policies: A History.* Washington, D.C.: Public Affairs Press, 1963.

Bouscaren, Anthony T. *International Migrations since 1945.* New York: Praeger, 1963.

Braybon, Gail, and Penny Summerfield. *Out of the Cage: Women's Experiences in Two World Wars.* New York: Pandora, 1987.

Bremner, Robert H., Minna Adams Hutcheson, and Lucille Stein Greenberg. "American Red Cross Services in the War Against the European Axis, Pearl Harbor to 1947." *The History of the American National Red Cross,* vol. 13. Washington, D.C.: The American Red Cross, 1950.

A Bride's Guide to the U.S.A. British Good Housekeeping Magazine and the United States Office of War Information, n.d.

Calder, Angus. *The People's War: Britain, 1939–45.* London: Panther Books, 1971.

Commager, Henry Steele, ed. *Immigration and American History.* Minneapolis: University of Minnesota Press, 1961.

Costello, John. *Love, Sex and War: Changing Values, 1939–45.* London: Collins, 1985.

Dinnerstein, Leonard, and David M. Reimers. *Ethnic Americans: A History of Immigration.* 3d ed. New York: Harper and Row, 1988.

Ellis, John. *The Sharp End of War: The Fighting Man in World War II.* New York: Scribners, 1980.

Enloe, Cynthia. *Does Khaki Become You? The Militarization of Women's Lives.* Boston: South End Press, 1983.

Erickson, Charlotte. *Invisible Immigrants: The Adaptation of English and Scottish Immigrants in Nineteenth-Century America.* Coral Gables, Fla.: University of Miami Press, 1972.

Fussell, Paul. *Wartime: Understanding and Behavior in the Second World War.* New York: Oxford University Press, 1989.

Gabaccia, Donna, ed. *Seeking Common Ground: Multidisciplinary Studies of Immigrant Women in the United States.* Westport, Conn.: Praeger, 1992.

Higonnet, Margaret Randolph, Jane Jenson, Sonya Michel, and Margaret Collins Weitz, eds. *Behind the Lines: Gender and the Two World Wars.* New Haven: Yale University Press, 1987.

Immigration and Naturalization Systems of the United States. Report of the Committee of the Judiciary (S.Res. 137). Washington, D.C.: Government Printing Office, April 1950.

Kaplan, Philip, and Rex Alan Smith. *One Last Look: A Sentimental Journey to the Eighth Air Force Heavy Bomber Bases of World War II in England.* New York: Abbeville Press, 1983.

Kellogg, Lt. Col. Albert B. *Marriages of Soldiers [of World War I].* Historical Section. Army War College, July 1942.

Kennett, Lee. *GI: The American Soldier in World War II.* New York: Warner, 1987.

Lee, Helene. *Bittersweet Decision.* Lockport, N.Y.: Roselee Publications, 1985.

Long, Vera Audrey Cracknell. *World War II Pilgrim Brides from Britain: "The Original GI Brides."* Vienna, Va.: By the author, 1988.

Longmate, Norman. *The G.I.s: The Americans in Britain, 1942–1945.* New York: Scribners, 1975.

Malkin, Richard. *Marriage, Morals and War.* New York: Arden, 1943.

Marwick, Arthur. *War and Social Change in the Twentieth Century: A Comparative Study of Britain, France, Germany, Russia, and the United States.* New York: St. Martin's, 1974.

Mead, Margaret. *The American Troops and the British Community: An Examination of the Relationship between American Troops and the British.* London: Hutcheson, 1944.

———. "The Yank in Britain." *Current Affairs* 64 (11 March 1944): 4–16.

Minns, Raynes. *Bombers and Mash: The Domestic Front, 1939–1945.* London: Virago, 1980.

Nevins, Allan, ed. *America: Through British Eyes.* New York: Oxford University Press, 1948.

Nord, Douglas C. "In Pursuit of 'Invisible' Immigrants: The Case of British Immigration to the United States." In *Contemporary American Immigration Interpretive Essays (European),* ed. Dennis Laurence Cuddy. The Immigrant Heritage of America Series. Boston: Twayne, 1982.

Reimers, David. *Still the Golden Door: The Third World Comes to America*. New York: Columbia University Press, 1992.

Reynolds, David. *Rich Relations: The American Occupation of Britain, 1942–1945.* London: HarperCollins, 1995.

Saywell, Shelley. *Women in War.* New York: Viking Penguin, 1985.

Seller, Maxine Schwartz, ed. *Immigrant Women.* Philadelphia: Temple University Press, 1981.

Shukert, Elfrieda Berthiaume, and Barbara Smith Scibetta. *War Brides of World War II*. Novato, Calif.: Presidio Press, 1988.

Simon, Rita James. *Public Opinion and the Immigrant: Print Media Coverage, 1880–1980*. Lexington, Mass.: Heath, 1985.

Simon, Rita James, and Caroline B. Brettell, eds. *International Migration: The Female Experience.* Totowa, N.J.: Rowman and Allanheld, 1986.

Sprague, Pfc. William F. *The Problems of Marriages in the European Theater of Operation.* Past Affairs Department, History Sub-section, ETOUSA, April 1944.

Special Services Division, Army Service Forces. *A Short Guide to Great Britain.* Washington, D.C.: War and Army Departments, 1942.

Summerfield, Penny. *Women Workers in the Second World War: Production and Patriarchy in Conflict.* London: Croom Helm, 1984.

Thernstrom, Stephan, ed. *Harvard Encyclopedia of American Ethnic Groups.* Cambridge, Mass.: Harvard University Press, 1980.

Virden, Jenel. "British War Brides of World War II: A Passing Fad with Post-War Complications." Master's thesis, Washington State University, 1983.

War Brides and Their Shipment to the United States. Occupation Forces in Europe Series, 1945–46. Office of the Chief Historian, Headquarters European Command. United States Army, 1947.

Weatherford, Doris. *Foreign and Female: Immigrant Women in America, 1840–1930*. New York: Schocken, 1986.

Wharton, Margaret. *Marlborough Revisited and the War Remembered: A G.I. Bride Looks Back*. Gloucester: Alan Sutton, 1987.

———. *Recollections of a GI War Bride: A Wiltshire Childhood.* Gloucester: Alan Sutton, 1984.

Winfield, Pamela. *Bye Bye Baby: The Story of the Children the GIs Left Behind.* London: Bloomsbury Publishing Ltd., 1992.

———. *Sentimental Journey: The Story of the GI Brides.* London: Constable, 1984.

Wordlow, Chester. "The Transportation Corps: Movements, Training, and Supply." *United States Army in World War II*. Washington, D.C.: Department of the Army, 1956.

Wyman, Mark. *Round-trip to America: The Immigrants Return to Europe, 1880–1930*. Ithaca: Cornell University Press, 1993.

Index

JENEL VIRDEN is a lecturer in the Department of American Studies at the University of Hull, England. She has published articles and presented papers about British immigration and military history.

Books in the Statue of Liberty–Ellis Island
Centennial Series

The Immigrant World of Ybor City: Italians and Their
Latin Neighbors in Tampa, 1885–1985   *Gary R. Mormino
and George E. Pozzetta*

The Butte Irish: Class and Ethnicity in an American
Mining Town, 1875–1925   *David M. Emmons*

The Making of an American Pluralism: Buffalo, New
York, 1825–60   *David A. Gerber*

Germans in the New World: Essays in the History of
Immigration   *Frederick C. Luebke*

A Century of European Migrations, 1830–1930   *Edited by
Rudolph J. Vecoli and Suzanne M. Sinke*

The Persistence of Ethnicity: Dutch Calvinist Pioneers in
Amsterdam, Montana   *Rob Kroes*

Family, Church, and Market: A Mennonite Community
in the Old and the New Worlds, 1850–1930
Royden K. Loewen

Between Race and Ethnicity: Cape Verdean American
Immigrants, 1860–1965   *Marilyn Halter*

Les Icariens: The Utopian Dream in Europe and America
Robert P. Sutton

Labor and Community: Mexican Citrus Worker Villages
in a Southern California County, 1900–1950
Gilbert G. González

Contented among Strangers: Rural German-Speaking
Women and Their Families in the Nineteenth-Century
Midwest   *Linda Schelbitzki Pickle*

Dutch Farmer in the Missouri Valley: The Life and
Letters of Ulbe Eringa, 1866–1950   *Brian W. Beltman*

Good-bye, Piccadilly: British War Brides in America
Jenel Virden